"*Notes to Myself* lit a path within. *Spiritual Notes to Myself* is a gentle guide to walking that path daily. It is filled with wisdom and joy."

— **Robert Johnson**, author of *He* and *She*

"*How to Live in the World and Still Be Happy* offers more than hope. It is a lifeline. Thank you, Hugh! You surely opened my eyes … again!"

— **Iyanla Vanzant**, author of
One Day My Soul Just Opened Up

"Hugh Prather has done it again. *Spiritual Notes to Myself* is a spiritual masterpiece. A classic for our times."

— **Richard Carlson**, author of
Don't Sweat the Small Stuff

"The gifts of wisdom and the treasured insights of Hugh Prather flow to us once again from the generosity of his Spirit in this wonderful book [*Shining Through*]."

— **Neale Donald Walsch**, author of
Conversations with God

"[*The Little Book of Letting Go* is] a treasure trove of practical, spiritual wisdom."

— **Joan Borysenko**, author of
Minding the Body, Mending the Mind

GENTLY DOWN
THIS DREAM

GENTLY DOWN THIS DREAM

Notes on My Sudden Departure

HUGH & GAYLE PRATHER

New World Library
Novato, California

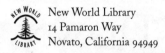 New World Library
14 Pamaron Way
Novato, California 94949

Text design by Tona Pearce Myers
Interior illustrations © Shutterstock.com

Library of Congress Cataloging-in-Publication data is available.

First printing, January 2023
ISBN 978-1-60868-841-8
Ebook ISBN 978-1-60868-842-5

Printed in Canada on 100% postconsumer-waste recycled paper

 New World Library is proud to be a Gold Certified Environmentally Responsible Publisher. Publisher certification awarded by Green Press Initiative.

10   9   8   7   6   5   4   3   2   1

CONTENTS

A Note to the Reader

Hugh and I worked on all his/our books together. Generally, he would write the first draft, and then, as he would often say, "Gayle would tell me how bad it was but that she could fix it." Despite his protestations, we had a truly loving collaboration, because we both wanted to express our shared belief in love, oneness, and peace. After I finished editing this most recent book, we laughed about my changes and additions and assumed that we would continue doing this for years to come. Hugh died the next day.

Because he is no longer here, I want to tell you more about how we wrote our books. Early on, we recognized that the books would be incredibly complicated to both write and read unless we generally had only one narrator, and since he was much better known than I, having him talk about me was both sensible and practical. Adding to this was the fact that neither one of us ever wanted to be famous or rich. We wanted to communicate that which we had recognized could keep marriages together and allow people to live in the world with love, peace, and forgiveness. Even though I was a feminist and believed strongly in women's rights, as did Hugh, being recognized as his equal partner in the publishing business was not important to me. And, I will add, Hugh accepted the fact that for several years, I refused to shave my legs...although I can no longer remember what that had to do with being a feminist.

Hugh was the love of my life; we went through so much together, and despite all the problems (and there were many), we love each other eternally. We were one, we are one, and in oneness there is no me.

When I reread this book, I realized how gentle and perfect it is for the divisive times in which we live, but also how different. Hugh recognized that the purpose of a spiritual path is not to make the world work the way we want it to but rather to learn to live with love, forgiveness, and peace in the world the way it is and, by doing this, to finally recognize what truly makes us happy.

At Hugh's memorial service, we sang "Row, Row, Row Your Boat," which was not only his favorite song but also an extraordinarily simple explanation for how to live peacefully in a world full of war, hatred, and separation. Rather than fighting against the current by trying to row upstream, we drift gently down into the peaceful waters of love and oneness. This is not denial about the tragedies in the world but instead the recognition that we accomplish far more healing for ourselves and everyone around us by acknowledging that our anger, our judgments, and our fears only add to separation. To row gently is to flow into the light of God, which is what Hugh did.

There is a magnificent truth at the heart of all great spiritual teachings, an eternal light that connects all of us. The things we think we need and want often only bring us fleeting moments of happiness. True happiness is eternal; it does not ebb and flow.

This new book also reminds me of Hugh's first book, *Notes to Myself*, which was published in 1970. That book was a highly personal work, and at its center was a message of hope that resonated with people around the world. I honestly believe that *Gently Down This Dream* could do the same thing. If you read this book with an open mind and a willing spirit, I believe you will understand what it means to truly live in peace.

Hugh died in 2010, and it is now 2022, so why did it take so long for the book to be published? Hugh and I briefly had a literary agent, but that was ages ago. I was unsure what to do. I definitely wanted the book to be published, but I sent it to only one company, and they very politely rejected it. You will be pleased to know that I quickly forgave them, and I assumed that it would never be published. While this made me sad, I accepted that the reality of business in this world is not always connected to that which might benefit others. And then something wonderful and amazing occurred!

In early 2020, I was contacted by Joe Durepos, a college student Hugh had met in Santa Fe many years before. Joe had read and loved *Notes to Myself*, and one day he found himself in a bookstore buying more copies of said book, and being in a hurry, he jumped in front of a man who was waiting to check out. The woman who happened to be at the counter commented on the fact that he had stepped in front of the man who wrote the books he was buying. Assuming that the gentleman would be upset, Joe turned around to apologize, but Hugh simply suggested that they go have lunch together, and so began a wonderful friendship.

As it turned out, after an amazing career as a bookseller and acquisitions editor, Joe was semiretired but working now as a literary agent! When we chatted, he asked if Hugh had written anything that had not been published. I sent him the manuscript, along with the following declaration: "And if you don't like the book, that's OK, too!" His immediate response was: "I already like it. ☺" In my heart, I know that Hugh was guiding this amazing and blessed reunion.

Joe made various editorial suggestions that included changing the title of the book to one that more accurately reflected the book's themes and who Hugh was. While Hugh did not and could not know that he would die the day after the book was finished, the subtitle — *Notes Upon My Sudden Departure* — is accurate, because Hugh had prepared for that event by making the peace of God more important than anything in this world. Hugh had learned to float gently down this dream, without fear, without worry, without trying to change that which we have no power over. This is at the heart of the book's message, and I believe Hugh's enduring hope for us all.

— Gayle Prather
Tucson, Arizona
March 2022

Rule One

Don't make things worse.

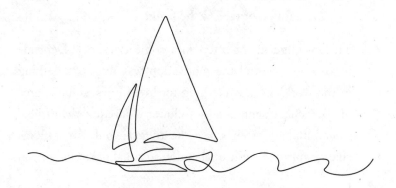

GENTLY DOWN THIS DREAM

Just because you row your boat gently down the stream, doesn't mean you get to control the scenery on the shore. What you do get are four merrilies for every three times you row.

When we experience peace, many of the harsher aspects of life begin to soften. Peace, however, does not manipulate specific people and events. It merely gives us a gentler attitude with which to deal with them.

One of the major impediments to spiritual progress is the thought that we deserve external rewards for walking a spiritual path. We want peace, *and* we want the world to work. But, of course, the world doesn't cooperate. Sooner or later, it becomes impossible to deny that simply because we try hard to do and be good, there are no specific outward effects we can count on or take to the bank.

This insight can, and often does, come as a shock. Depending on how central the motivation was to get something in the world, even something for loved ones, some degree of disenchantment usually follows. Consequently, disillusioned students often believe that there are only two options: change spiritual paths or abandon spiritual paths altogether.

Our spiritual journey can come in countless forms, but at the heart of each is a belief in love. There would be no Golden

Rule running through all the world's great religions if in the back of our minds we didn't know that we share a common humanity. After giving its version, the Talmud states, "This is the law. All the rest is commentary."

Students of a spiritual path embrace oneness as a core belief, even though they may not use that word to describe it. But if their path is just one of the many tools they use to deal with the daily grind, it will gradually lose its value. In fact, in due course it will be seen as an ineffectual and unreliable tool only to be tried as a last resort.

We are *always* practicing the Golden Rule. Or at least the principle behind the rule: What we do to others, we do to ourselves. If we treat another destructively, we cannot escape being destructive to ourselves. Yet it is also true that the ways we attack ourselves will be reflected in the ways we attack others. The outward forms of the attack may differ, but the essence of the attack is the same.

Whether through prayer, meditation, affirmation, or positive thinking, most people feel a tinge of anxiety whenever they try to use spiritual truth as a means of getting what they want. In my opinion, this discomfort comes from the awareness that we are betraying our basic nature.

When things go well, we think our path is working, but if they go poorly, we think it's failing. Taking up a spiritual path seems difficult because it asks us to respond to "all things" equally, to respond without judgment, and this goes against lifelong habits.

Because injustice and tragedy are not the same as mundane events, a leap of faith is required. We are asked to bridge *both* with love. This can only be done if we accept that spiritual truth is not worldly truth. Truth can only be experienced directly. And therein lies the difficulty. The day will appear to conspire against any spiritual truth we attempt to apply to what is not truly spiritual. Another way of saying this is that we must love without calculation.

To try to use spiritual truths to get what we think we need or deserve in life actually blocks the experience of truth, because it is based on inequality. It is the belief that if we are in possession of the right concepts, we have an advantage over those who don't know them.

If truth is true, it applies equally to the illiterate, the wealthy, the mentally impaired, the sick, the healthy, the insane, and the prisoner in solitary confinement. A truth that does not apply to everyone is not in harmony with the Golden Rule. Nor can it bring lasting happiness, because the mind is constantly leaning into the future, asking itself what it is not getting, instead of leaning back into the present.

Love — not how the day goes — is the most powerful determiner of happiness. The world cannot be controlled through positive thinking, but if we seek the Divine simply to have a deeper experience of the Divine, a beautiful purification of the mind begins and, increasingly, going through the day is like rowing gently down a river of peace.

Awakening

Awakening is a matter of persistence and starting over. There is not some spectacular moment when it all comes together. Awakening is eased into a little at a time. Like being cradled by a mother who gently wakes her baby from a long nap, you blink and slowly open your eyes to a smiling face, and to arms that you realize were there all along.

Dare to Be Ordinary

The world challenges you to be special and set apart. Dare instead to be ordinary. It doesn't matter whether the call is to be one up or one down, the victor or the vanquished, the essence of the call is to be different. Love sees all as one, for love *is* one. Ordinary love for ordinary people transforms a place of strife into a part of heaven.

BINKLEY

This is inspired by Binkley. He has become my kitty muse. Binkley is a twelve-year-old gray tabby. Our son John rescued him from his college dorm, in the sense that he caught him and told us we were to take care of him. There was strong evidence that as he wandered from room to room, he was partaking of illegal substances. Or at least inhaling them.

At the time we had two other beloved pets, a Siamese named KJ and a Shih Tzu–Chihuahua mix named Chocolate Mousse Pie. Both were characters. KJ would steal any workman's tools, Gayle's mom's brassieres, and other odds and ends and hide them in his lair. And Mousse had a vocabulary of snorts, sneezes, coughs, and barks that kept us all laughing.

Then Binkley arrived.

We took him to a vet to get checked out, and Binkley bit her. And he has bitten every other vet we have since gone to. We now have to tranquilize him first.

When strangers come over, Binkley slyly sneaks up and nips them on their legs until they pet him. His sneakiness is ingenious, executed through a series of slow stretches and rolls. Knowing we will put him up as soon as someone comes through the front door, Binkley has mastered the hidden ambush. The older we get, the more successful this out-of-sight, out-of-mind tactic has become.

To this day Binkley has never learned to use a litter box. He gets in it but hangs his backside out the opening. He never grooms himself. He shreds rugs and furniture. He frequently eats too fast and throws up. And if we are headed in the direction of the kitchen, he runs between our legs and tries to trip us. Our floors are tile.

But our biggest test came when Binkley would go after KJ. Even though this happened only every month or two, it was so distressing to our family that we ended up keeping the cats in separate parts of the house.

Needless to say, Binkley didn't become the favorite family pet.

Yet once Mousse and KJ died, he became our only pet. At that point Gayle and I realized we had an opportunity. We could atone for our erratic devotion to the many pets we had had before by devoting ourselves to Binkley.

Animals often supply pet owners with what might be called the preschool level of learning how to walk a spiritual path. One could say that infants provide the kindergarten level of spiritual learning, because the demands are more numerous and complicated. Yet in both cases the opportunity to express a very direct and simple form of love is undeniable.

Kittens and puppies, as well as cats and dogs, are so obviously innocent that few people can avoid seeing that the nature of the relationship rests entirely in their hands. We are there to give. They are there to receive. Clearly the same is true of infants, but since I touch on children in several other places, let's stick with pets.

Finding ourselves in a situation that demands pure giving, and choosing to carry out that demand day in and day out, imparts a miracle. For some, it is their first. Despite everything we have learned about the rewards of getting (and we have all learned that lesson well), we suddenly experience the impossible. We can be a pure giver and receive not only as much as we give, but *more*. That isn't the way the world is supposed to work.

Of course, that's the way most religious philosophies say it works, but come on now, how many people do you know who actually practice the Golden Rule in any consistent way? How many people do you know who put the happiness of others first? Even the happiness of their own partners? Whether in business, politics, or finding a parking place, the world believes deeply that we are naive, possibly even self-destructive, if we are not self-serving.

But now comes along a little animal that is simply itself. It does what it does. And we may find it funny, or time-consuming, or adorable, or willful, or affectionate, or annoying, or all of the above. But if we are honest, it is undeniably innocent, and therefore we understand that our attitudes toward our pet are of our own making.

I recognize that many pet owners fail to see their pets as a spiritual opportunity. Many project their own weaknesses onto their pets and see them as anything but innocent. In their eyes, the pet becomes a version of themselves. They attribute blameworthy attributes to what is merely a little animal.

In our forty-five-year marriage Gayle and I have had many pets, and in the first fifteen or so years we failed our animals in several ways. Although we took good care of them while they were with us, some — because of allergies one of our boys had, or because of an "intolerable" trait that would develop, or because of not being able to take a pet to where we were moving (who ever uses such an excuse to rid themselves of their child?) or other essentially selfish motives (the allergies being the one exception) — we were much too quick to find them "another home." As a result, two or three ended up in homes where they were neglected. These memories are heartbreaking to both of us.

Naturally there are changes in life circumstances that require a pet's accommodations be altered, such as deaths, divorces, and transfers with rigid parameters. But trivial excuses are not difficult to discern.

Once we acknowledged our less-than-sensitive patterns, we resolved to treat all future pets with love and care and to make a lifelong commitment to each one.

Which brings me back to Binkley. After a few adjustments, such as finding a safe way to walk toward the kitchen, we were left with the bundle of traits already described, plus one more that is immensely important. Binkley, like most cats, loves to be petted. An added bonus, since he has a year-round, fast-growing undercoat that requires daily brushing, is that he also likes to be groomed. By "fast," we're talking *Guinness Book of Records* fast.

God is love. And I believe that our function in life is to represent God's love. The most powerful way to do this is to hold people in our prayers, but there is a loving way to do almost anything.

As we go through the day, we usually have a number of little encounters with tech-support people, clerks, coworkers, waitstaff, individuals in line, other drivers, other shoppers, and so on. In each of these meetings we leave something behind. Often it is indifference or mere politeness or preoccupation. But sometimes it is something that comes from a better part of us.

This better thing we leave behind does not have to be overt. We don't have to smile or make a joke or strike up a conversation. Many times, the exchange can be merely a sincere and silent blessing. But those are felt, just as unspoken impatience or condemnation can be felt.

So, by the end of a day, we have left a trail, and it is within our power to make that trail one of gentleness, love, and kindness.

Binkley is one of the ways Gayle and I practice this pure and simple form of love. One of the first things we do in the morning and last things we do at night is simply to love Binkley. Binkley, it turns out, can count to two, so he loudly lets us know if one of us has forgotten.

I mentioned pets as preschool. For me it works this way. As I pet and groom Binkley, I say to myself, *God is love. I am here to represent God's love for you.* And I try to stay focused on just that one thought — petting Binkley as I imagine God would pet Binkley. And if my thoughts wander, I bring them back to love.

After many months of doing this, it has become a template for the attitude I try to have toward those I encounter or who cross my mind each day. I probably don't have to add that Binkley has changed, also — from a lot of trouble to a remarkable blessing in my life, even though all his behaviors remain admirably intact.

Asking for Help

Taking responsibility should not become a form of rigid, closed-minded self-sufficiency. Simply do this: close your eyes and say, "Please help me." To ask for help from that which is greater than us relaxes our minds and hearts. It acknowledges that there is One who is here to help. And it is an act of faith that help will indeed become apparent.

Almost all great spiritual teachers have distinguished between God and the world. God is without limits. The perceptual world is nothing but limits. It therefore makes no sense at all to seek to use God for personal gain in the world, to seek the Unlimited in order to receive more of the limited. We seek God for more God, not more world, and to try to do both is not to seek God at all.

There is an eternal flame of Truth, a light that can never be extinguished. It is with us now and here. Its brilliance embraces us, and nothing exists that can threaten it or change it in any way. Fear is often a projection into the future, but to turn away from what *might* happen to what is *always* happening opens our eyes to this invulnerable beauty and holiness. Asking for help acknowledges that Love itself is the light in which we stand.

You Always Know
What to Do

God does not stand in the corner and mumble. You are not called upon to read hidden signs and indicators. There is not some code that God is asking you to break, whereby if you are successful, you will then know what to do. You always know what to do in the present, because God is peace. You have a peaceful preference right now. Simply follow it. Pause, see it, and act with assurance. Do not look back and question the thing you felt peaceful about doing. Stopping and turning to peace was a holy act. Honor it, and trust each new step you take in peace.

Have a Little Faith

These are times when faith in government, the economy, relationships, our health, and almost every category we can think of seems unwarranted. And it is. But it has always been unwarranted. The world, being based on separation, is a place where each small thing has its own agenda. It is simply too chaotic to be relied on.

Knowing that anything can change at any moment can generate great fear, and we obviously live in a time of deep universal anxiety. The future stretches before us like a minefield. Yet there is something more to reality than uncertainty, and faith opens our eyes to it.

Faith is a different kind of effort than we are accustomed to making. It is more a not doing than a doing. It is more a letting go than a determination to control. It is a falling back into arms we somehow know are there but we have little, or no, outward evidence even exist. It is a decision to trust.

No one lacks faith. We would be immobilized without it. Every action we take, every sentence we think, is based on faith in *something*. We have faith in the images we hold of ourselves. We have faith in how we have characterized certain people and events. We have faith in what the rest of the day will be like. We have faith that we have made mistakes and that we know what they are. Faith is based on the past, yet it has meaning only because we have faith the future will bear us out.

The phrase "take a leap of faith" points to another kind of faith. It is to jump without a net. It is to respond to a gentle inner nudge, knowing that we may have misinterpreted.

How often we put aside our faith in a peaceful intuition because it conflicts with our past-based faith! It happened to me just this week. I have always been interested in accents and in trying to place them. I was talking to a man with an unusual accent. It sounded like he could have come from Boston, but that wasn't quite it. I had an intuition that I shouldn't ask him about it, but I reasoned away my faith in the intuition and asked him anyway. He said, "Oh, you're talking about my accent. I have a speech impediment." This was very awkward, but he was nice and said he got that question a lot. If I had had more faith in my intuition, I would have avoided the awkwardness.

There is indeed "a still small voice," but my need is to have more faith in it, because it speaks as clearly to life decisions as to seemingly innocent conversational comments. The voice is ever present, but my faith in it is sporadic, and I am determined to change that.

In my opinion, faith in what the *past* has taught us about our identity, the direction we are headed, who should and should not be in our lives — even our faith in what we think we know about God and Truth — can all be safely laid aside. And should be laid aside repeatedly. We need hold on to nothing. Over and over, we should take a leap into boundless and endless stillness. We should open our hearts, let go completely, and have faith.

STUMBLING

It's better to stumble over a fact than to step around it. Some of the most helpful facts are the ones we didn't see coming. When we find ourselves facedown, the fact now has our attention. If it weren't for stumbling, we would never find our way home.

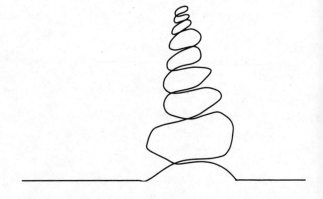

Cheerfulness

In memorial services we sometimes hear the thought that those of us in grief should be happy that we had this person for the time we did. That's a little like saying, "Now that you have lost your job, your money, and your house, you should feel grateful that you had them for as long as you did."

Naturally it's good to celebrate the lives of the deceased and to remind ourselves of the positive examples they gave, as well as to see that we have the opportunity to embody those finer qualities ourselves. For many people, it is also helpful to remember that they remain with us to help us accomplish just that. This is honest and self-affirming and, if we follow through, can even be transformational.

At the moment, the world is not a very happy place, if indeed it ever was. But it seems that today fear, unhappiness, and bitterness are uniquely widespread. Many are experiencing an almost constant background of hopelessness and depression. For some, the problem is more severe: a sense of looming catastrophe.

One merely has to look around to see that there is substantial evidence to support these feelings, and we do ourselves a disservice to try to deny this reality or to cheer each other up. Cheerfulness can't be forced on ourselves or others, and the attempt to do so can split our mind so that we are conflicted about who we truly are and what we are feeling; we vacillate between thinking of ourselves as happy and whole, only to doubt that as soon as another difficulty presents itself. One can be distracted from fear for only limited periods, and when the distraction fades, discouragement and despair can return with even greater force.

That said, it's also true that going through the day in a good mood makes life easier — provided we are not trying to impose our mood on others. A bad mood can contain an element of coercion. Individuals in a funk often find those who are happy annoying. "Misery loves company" is only partially true. Misery not only feels more comfortable around the miserable; it also includes the unconscious intent to bring other people down to its level. That is why a simple change in purpose, such as *I will now be kind*, can of itself undercut ill humor.

Fortuitous circumstances can put one in a good mood, but it's a mistake to think that's what is always needed. Clearly there are people who are innately cheerful who do not try to pressure those around them to share their outlook. Little children frequently display this attitude. Surprisingly often, they are happy for no apparent reason. Whether adult or child, we give everything we see the meaning it has for us. Innately cheerful individuals perceive, think, and react more gently. This may be a basic part of a person's nature, but it also can be learned through practice.

More progress is made in the long run if one does not set the goal of jumping from dour to lighthearted in a single day. Merely set the goal of being a little more peaceful, a little happier, a little more amused at the start of each activity. The more modest the goal, the more effective it tends to be. The mind can smile. Did you know that? Try it now.

Which brings us to the question of whether it is possible to make another person happy. Trying to force cheerfulness is not the same as using one's intuition to relate to an individual in a more harmonious way. For example, there's no doubt that we know exactly what to say or do to make our partner unhappy, angry, or anxious — a capacity we display skillfully during most arguments. That ability is based on insight, but the insight is used negatively. This same knowledge of our partner can also be used to make them feel safer, more comfortable, more appreciated — in short, happier. Trite as it may seem, doing so invariably lightens our mood as well.

The Real Meaning of Love

If it's important to you, it's important to me. What other meaning could love have?

Mother's Day and the Golden Rule

It was Saturday afternoon, the day before Mother's Day.

I was working out ("working out" sounds better than "sitting on a stationary bike in underwear watching a *Dexter* rerun") when suddenly our dog Mousse started barking.

This meant someone was at the front door. But I was in my underwear and also doing what no truly spiritual person should do — watching a show about a serial killer who only kills bad guys.

So, like the coward I am, I ran to the front door and peeked through the peeking window to see if this was a human being truly worthy of my time. All I saw was a young woman walking back to her delivery truck.

When the truck was out of sight, I cracked the door to see what package had been left, but there was none.

Oh well.

I got back on the bike, and a little later Mousse started barking again.

Again, the peeking. But this time, as she headed back to her truck, I could see she was holding a large gift basket.

Oh my God. A Mother's Day gift.

I knew it was too late in the day for her to be coming back and that it would probably not be delivered on Sunday. And she was about to drive off.

Embarrassment, versus my wife's happiness.

I bolted out the door, stopped her just in time, grabbed the basket, and said, "Wait a second. I want to give you a tip."

Too shocked to answer, she just stood there. I ran back in the house, got more cash than the gift basket itself probably cost, and shoved it in her hand.

My idea was to give her a tip so large that it would erase the memory of a senior citizen in underwear. I like to think she mentioned it to no one when she got back to Gift Baskets "R" Us.

There are decisions we have time to think through and decisions we don't. (*Do I damage the car or hit the baby quail? Really no time to weigh consequences.*)

The choice to put another's happiness above our own embarrassment or inconvenience is generally an easy decision to make. Other problems can be more difficult.

CURING CLUSTER MISTAKE SYNDROME

There are classic addictions such as alcohol, drugs, smoking, gambling, and so on, but there's another category that functions in a similar way that is not readily seen as an addiction by society. It is a combination of several small addictions that work in unison with an equally destructive force.

A given individual might, for example, periodically drink too much and drive; occasionally gamble to excess; go on spending sprees now and then, resulting in unnecessary credit-card debt; or eat food known to be physically harmful. These individual activities may not be frequent or extreme enough to stand out as classic addictions, but they have a cumulative, debilitating effect. I'll refer to the aggregate as "cluster mistake syndrome" (CMS — destined to appear in an upcoming drug ad).

The question that the classically addicted must ask is the same one required of individuals with CMS: *Why, knowing that a behavior is misguided, do I proceed to do it anyway?* What unifying impulse underlies these activities?

In the case of those who are patently addicted, as with those with CMS, we choose to give preference to the ego (the darker, agitated side of our mind). And in both cases the behavior tends to escalate over time.

This preference can have differing motivations. For example, individuals may increase the destructive behavior because they have *consciously* chosen to side with their baser instincts — and a surprising number of us have done just that. In pursuit of some self-serving goal, they are willing, sometimes eager, to betray their loved ones, themselves, and God or whatever name they use for spiritual potential. These individuals usually believe deeply in their superiority.

Another impetus for escalating mistakes is a desire to be "honest" with themselves as a means of being at war with their own inner darkness, which in fact they often have some insight into. But the honesty is basically self-abasement, and each battle can become a doomed struggle. You can't argue or reason yourself out of what you truly believe, and to attempt to do so merely reinforces the destructive belief because you are operating from a position of weakness. Sometimes this dynamic is further fueled by the thought: *I'll keep making this mistake until things get so bad, I'll want to quit.* One of this dynamic's symptoms is the desire to be a victim.

Alternatively, the person who has decided to devote themselves to their darkness may for a time feel relatively limited remorse, few second thoughts, and little or no anguish. They simply go on sharpening their egos and can become quite good at destroying other people's lives.

Most individuals don't fall into either category. They spend their lives randomly vacillating between their ego and their divinity, and never make a deep commitment to either, except perhaps in the final weeks or months of their lives.

A single mistake, or a cluster of mistakes, only requires correction. Nothing more. Dwelling on guilt does not correct. Unquestionably we all love to define other people's weaknesses and to paint a thick coat of grievances on just about everyone.

Most of us keep a running list of our mistakes and continue adding to it. This is a cherished human practice. It seems humble. It seems honest. But endlessly rewriting what should have happened does not correct. Projecting the likelihood of future mistakes does not correct. However, when we persist in looking for and finding what there is to value within ourselves, we discover a pure and loving being. This then allows us to see ourselves in others. Now we are operating from strength. "Love thy neighbor as thyself" is the great transformative potential we all possess.

Your Partner

Your partner is your equal; get over it.

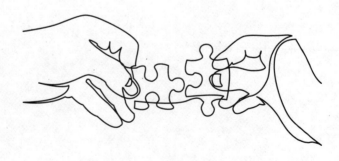

JENNY AND JANE

Jenny wrote aggressively researched essays that landed her in Advanced Placement.

Jane, Jenny's younger sister, liked playing "I'm going to get your bone" with her beloved whippet.

Jenny brushed out her gloriously long hair every night until it shone like redemption.

Jane did little with her hair, but when she was bored, she allowed Jenny to "clip and trim."

Jenny became the youngest girl ever chosen captain of the Quiz Bowl team and took her high school to the state semi-finals.

Jane would not pretend that she had not heard their ancient, tall, and talkative neighbor call her name, and she would laugh at the same stories he had told a hundred times.

Jenny was admired by her family, her teachers, and several of her friends.

Jane was happy. Which worried her parents.

YOUR TEENAGER

Your teenager is your moral and intellectual equal — and knows it.

Controlling Another

Try to control anyone and you instantly lose whatever peace you had. Even the unspoken *desire* to pressure someone turns the mind against itself the instant the thought forms.

The Gifts of Growing Older

Although it's hard for people who know me to believe, I went through a good-looking phase. I have pictures to prove it. A full head of hair. The illusion of a waistline. A cleft chin with no mini-chin below.

I worked hard to stretch out my moment of hirsute hunki-ness. I did bench presses, ran mega miles, applied Rogaine, and wore blue contacts.

The mirror was my friend. But then midlife kicked in, and it began to betray me. These days, my mirror and I don't see much of each other, although if my vision gets any worse, I may be able to forgive it.

On the body, everything either sticks out or hangs down. Old age is when it all hangs down. Body parts scream "Get me out of here!" and try to jump overboard. Earlobes plunge toward the shoulders, the chest lands on the stomach, and the stomach stretches so far down that it's hard to tell the sex of some naked seniors. Fortunately, no one wants to see a naked senior.

Clearly, it's discourteous to grow old, a sign of ill breeding. Furthermore, it's an assault on young people's sensibilities. But since it's a fairly common fault, you would think that our culture would cut us all a little slack…or a lot. But it doesn't. The media and entertainment industries treat aging as not only a blunder but a horror. "Fran Fabulous just turned fifty. My four-year-old saw her on TV and hid in the closet." Old people just shouldn't do that to children.

I'm sure it's for the children's sake that, for the most part, people past a certain age are kept off TV. If inhabitants of another planet were able to pick up our TV signals, they would assume that 80 percent of Earth's population was between the ages of eighteen and forty. Movies, books, talk shows, and the like focus on the body's brief blooming period. Even old people don't want to look at old people.

Clearly, it's a mistake to grow old, but once that mistake is made, it's an even greater mistake to fight it. We have a friend who is so fixated on trying to look young that her friends joke that whenever her plastic surgeon has a cancellation, he calls her. She has had everything on her body redone except her navel. She is not a happy person. If she could just accept that she, like all her friends and family, is aging, she would at least have the chance of a little peace of mind.

Unless one's occupation is tied to looking young, trying to freeze the body in time is a pointless battle. It is happier to relax and be carried along on the same tide as everyone else.

As it gets harder to sleep, the one who lies beside you gets noisier. That's just the way it is. As taste buds die off and food begins to taste like cardboard, aging intestines force you to eat an ever-blander diet. That's just the way it is. As balance becomes more of a problem, the bones become more brittle. It's all so unfair, but that's just the way it is.

I'm beginning to notice a few unexpected benefits from looking my age. I am anonymous. I am invisible. I can move down a crowded grocery aisle like a ghost. I never did have any fashion sense, but now I don't feel guilty for not putting more effort into my wardrobe. Most of my shirts and all my pants are basically the same color — but no one notices. I can put on a few pounds or drop a few — no one remembers what I looked like before.

As our preoccupation with our bodies lessens, we find that we can devote our minds to other things, like trying to be a better spouse, parent, grandparent, sibling, and friend. Aging offers us a choice. We can become bitter, or we can become gentler, kinder. If we can walk in gentleness and kindness, the world becomes a more welcoming place to live, regardless of our age or our aches and pains.

WHAT DO YOU BELIEVE?

As we amble along our chosen path, we encounter many distractions. One of the most insidious is the notion that to pursue a path is sufficient, that pursuit is an end in itself.

A few years ago, we were invited to do a two-day retreat sponsored by a wealthy organization that once a year invited some individual or group to edify them. In their invitation they made a point of characterizing themselves as "seekers of truth." That should have been a red flag, because we had run across organizations with similar aims, but this one paid awfully well.

We opened the first day with the invitation to interrupt us at any time with comments or questions. We then proceeded to talk about our spiritual beliefs and practices, and we demonstrated with a volunteer couple just how easily an issue can be resolved when the couple switched from their ego minds to their connected mind.

We walked the couple through the steps and, sure enough, it worked just as we had said it would.

So, there we were, talking about the difference between the chattering mind and the quiet mind and demonstrating fairly dramatically the practical implications of being aware of both, when the questions and comments started coming.

The remarks were all over the place, comparing our philosophy to past speakers' beliefs, questioning that we had made certain basic assumptions, disagreeing with how we had worded certain points, and all in all rejecting anything we had said with certainty. One person commented, "You aren't very dynamic. We've heard all of this before." Although he did add that the demonstration with the couple was "interesting."

The second day we had the group sit in a circle, and we asked each person: "What do you think is true? What are the basic truths that you can always rely on? What truths do you try to live by?"

This spurred numerous questions about what we meant by "truth." We tried to answer as simply and in as few words as we could, saying things like "We just want to know what you think is real and lasting, the facts about reality that you know you can rely on." This then brought on questions about what was "reality," but eventually we were able to get answers from all but two people in the circle.

Out of a group of about forty, only five people said that they believed in a lasting reality or truth, and they mentioned God, Spirit, inner guidance, time, life, conscience, and death. The other comments were mostly expressions of political and social responsibility, with a few continuing to argue against the worth of the exercise.

Naturally, each of us has our own individual process or path, and Gayle's and mine clearly are not a good fit for many people. However, what this long-standing and apparently sated group was challenging was not the merit of our answers but the fact that we *had* answers.

With a few exceptions, the individual members had convinced themselves that it is better to seek than to find. They were offended that we had settled on a way that was best for us. If your purpose is to "seek the truth," finding the truth pulls the meaning of your life out from under you.

The beliefs that Gayle and I try to live by are quite simple. In fact, we have noticed that they become simpler the longer we work at practicing them. Our prayers now are often only two or three words long. Sometimes only one. Sometimes just stillness. But we find that we stop and calm our minds several times a day. Aside from starting each day with a meditation, we don't follow a set schedule but simply pause whenever we get caught up in something trivial, which happens remarkably often.

In our opinion, it is not how many ways you have of stating the truth but how committed you are to carrying it out moment by moment that determines progress. Many people become obsessed with looking for ever better statements of truth rather than practicing what they already know.

And we all know enough. We know enough to get us through today. Whether it's the Sermon on the Mount, the Golden Rule, the Twelve Steps, or simply the desire to be kind to those we encounter and think of, any of those approaches — plus thousands of others that are simple, familiar, and much used — is sufficient.

Sit quietly and ask yourself what you believe. Do you want to be a better person today than you were yesterday? Then that is enough. Do you notice that you are happier when you are kind rather than controlling? Then that is enough. Do you find that the harsh circumstances of the world soften a little when you meditate? Then that is enough.

Anything that comes up today, anything at all, cannot block you from having a degree of peace if you will simply look into your heart, see what you believe, and practice it. That is a path based on truth. And the beauty it leads you toward becomes increasingly apparent the longer you walk it.

GREED

Extend grace to those who are greedy. They are not jeopardizing their afterlife but rather their knowledge of the kingdom of heaven within them now.

Dealing with Anger

Sometimes "a soft answer turneth away wrath," and sometimes it just annoys the hell out of the person.

If someone is determined to be angry, no matter how peaceful you are, they will probably stay angry. It took me way too long to learn that if I find myself under verbal attack, or in the presence of someone who is passive-aggressive, or around a person who just flat-out doesn't like me, it's best to extricate myself as quickly and unmemorably as possible.

I think of this as vanishing into peace, a kind of spiritual fadeaway. You slip away rather than slink away.

Naturally there are situations — for example, at work — where withdrawal is not an option. In these cases, it helps to minimize contact and shorten conversations as much as possible.

Except in extreme cases, breaking off all contact with a family member is also problematic. In a sense, we are composed of our family. We may think that we have renounced a parent, sibling, or grandparent, but their place in our mind has not been eradicated. So, the question becomes what effect we want this part of our mind to have on us.

It is possible to withdraw from a hostile encounter without judgment. *This person is angry. Being around them right now calls to my ego. To protect my mind, I will back away.* As I say, it's *possible*, but I don't always pull that off. Sometimes I feel an urgent desire to respond in kind, and do so, even though I inevitably regret it. This is especially true when the anger seems justified. But is there ever a time when anger doesn't seem justified?

Gayle and I and one of our sons were in a restaurant recently. By luck of the draw, we got the passive-aggressive server. She was so exquisitely sweet that we were instantly on guard. But she surprised us. We had no idea anyone could so masterfully ruin a dining experience. The topic we discussed at our table — we had a brain-decomposing length of time to do so — was whether she was conscious of her motivations. The vote was two yeses, one no.

During one half-hour stretch, during which time she was conversing with friends, I approached the manager and pointed out that the restaurant was now empty and we still did not have our food. He told me that the server had said we did not want it brought out until "the lady" had finished her salad. I assured him no such request had been made and that, furthermore, she had finished her salad twenty minutes ago. He pointed to Gayle's plate. "She still has some lettuce left."

At this point we had several choices. We could see how funny this was. We could ask for our food. We could pay for the salad and leave. Or we could get angry. Sadly, we chose the latter.

Then we made a second mistake. We treated the server with undeniable coolness for the rest of the meal. Judging by how the other servers looked over at us when she talked to them, her response was to discuss our table with her peers, thus encircling us in a ring of disapproval.

Feeling guilty, we left her a 25 percent tip.

This happened three days ago, and occasionally I still have to stop and let it go. Anger cements misery in place. It makes expressing our better nature in other encounters more difficult. And unless released entirely, it precludes peace of mind.

Acting out an unkind impulse only complicates the situation. It pushes the other person to become defensive and to react. Now the encounter takes on a life of its own, sometimes ensnaring other people, who in turn react. On the other hand, if we don't act out, if we simply withdraw, the effects of the encounter stay within our control, because they stay in our mind.

It Only Takes
a Little Kindness

When we look deep within ourselves, we are surprised to discover the mistake of thinking that we are alone. Our very "nature" is not alone. It only takes a little kindness to see within us "the better angels of our nature." This is the same host of angels that unfold their gentle wings around us. We are loved both inside and out.

Empathy

Empathy is not giving up part of yourself. It is the recognition that because you are deeply connected to this other living being, you are greater than yourself.

BEING RIGHT

The urge to be right is the urge to be separate.

POLITICS

Kindness is more important than party affiliation. Inner peace is more important than politics. Elections are not a free pass to become judgmental. Do you really think that God cares about your political opinions?

Sorry Seems to Be the Hardest Word

One Saturday morning, a man I will call Leo had to borrow his wife's car because his was in the shop. He went to the mall to get a battery for his watch. When he came out, the car was gone. He immediately called the police and within a few hours had filed a police report and an insurance claim. To do this he had to take taxis to various locations and spent over two hundred dollars in fares and tips, which he and his wife could little afford.

When he got home that evening, he told his wife what had happened.

"I have two questions," she said. "Why didn't you call Mother and have her chauffeur you around? And did you check the parking lot on the other side of the mall?"

"No. That's not where I parked it. And you know how critical your mother is."

"You think Mother is a judgmental person?"

"She is when it comes to me. And a few other people. Well, a lot of other people."

His wife didn't answer. Angrily, she called her mother and asked if she could pick them up and take them to the mall.

You guessed it. His wife's car was on the other side of the mall. Leo had walked out the wrong entrance. Now was the time for him to apologize.

But as the three of them stood there looking at the car, the circumstances were not ideal. His wife just shook her head as if to say, "You're an idiot." And his mother-in-law whispered to her in that tone that means, "I told you not to marry him."

Leo did apologize, then and there, and did so profusely. But then he made a common and ruinous mistake. He didn't put a period at the end of the apology. On the way home, when he and his wife were alone, he tried to justify not calling his mother-in-law. He said it had occurred to him to call, but he was afraid it would give her more ammunition against him. And he reminded her that she herself had said that her mother was judgmental.

This led to a shouting match, not to forgiveness.

Leo was right that his mother-in-law was against him (although he broke the ancient rule "I can criticize my parents, but you can't"). He was also right that calling her would have given her ammunition. But all that was irrelevant — if his purpose was to apologize.

Apology is a powerful and underutilized tool. But it must be pure to be effective. It won't always heal a rift in a relationship, but it can be the start of healing.

Apologizing, like any form of communication, can be over-used. When we do this, we may have slipped into the role of victim. We keep apologizing as a form of self-defense and counterattack. "I have done everything I can: I have apologized over and over. You are unfair because you won't accept it."

The qualified apology is also a mistake. And still another is to think that an apology is all that's needed and that, once it's given, the burden has shifted to the one who received it.

A real apology comes from empathy, not fear. Its purpose is to increase oneness. If given sincerely, it is without expectation. It is a gift of peace that comes from peace.

Wisdom

Not every battle must be fought to its bitter end.

An End in Itself

When you started your spiritual path, so did your ego.

Possibly you can always tell a spiritual thought from an ego thought, but for many people their path can slowly be taken over by their ego. Once this happens, it can be difficult to undo, because the individual loses the ability to distinguish between thoughts that sound spiritual and thoughts that come from what might be called their conscience or peaceful mind. Increasingly they learn to disguise destructive behavior under a mantle of goodness, and they end up fooling themselves as well as others.

How do you know when this is beginning to happen or has already happened? Only honest observation of the actual effect you are having on other people, especially those you are most intimately connected to, will give you the proof you need, because reasoning alone is no longer reliable.

If you think this has happened, a good first step is to stop talking to yourself. Words alone can no longer guide you, because you don't really know your true motive for what you are telling yourself. What is needed now is openness and stillness. In humility you must turn to the Light of God, to Truth, to Love, to the one, holy, sacred Reality, which is your Self and will always be your Self.

The key is humility. Only humility allows you to turn in a radically different direction. This turning is a wordless act. And you must not ask yourself if it is working. Or if you feel anything this time. Or whether you are making progress. Only the ego wants to judge progress. And you must not talk about your progress with other people. What you are doing is sacred, and you must hold it gently and quietly in your heart.

Those on a true spiritual path simply continue being peaceful and kind. They know there is no finish line they are heading toward, a place where they will arrive and can stop. What they are doing daily is an end in itself. It is *the* end in itself.

TIME

Time is a luxury. And unlike other luxuries, we have more than enough of it. Yet we are always doing what we don't need to be doing *now*. Thus, we discard large nuggets of this great potential comfort called time.

The solution is to luxuriate. Indulge yourself in time. Heap it on every instant.

Notice that the moment we get in a rush, we lose our peace. For example, we love to start projects late in the day, resulting in a rush to get to bed. That sense of rush is taken not only into sleep; there is often a residue of rush felt when we awake.

We also love to cut it short in the morning instead of giving ourselves more than enough time to get ready. And what does it mean to "get ready"? It entails washing, grooming, and dressing our bodies. Our goal is not really to get ready but to look ready.

But are *we* ready? Is our mind ready? Did we even look at the state of our mind as long as we looked in the mirror? No, we say, we don't have time for a moment of mental preparation. We'll make sure that both shoes are on, but we know not the direction we want to walk.

We got to work but not in peace. We got to the meeting but not in peace. We ran errands but not in peace. And throughout the day we "saved" time, for that was our unacknowledged goal. The unasked question was, for what did we save it?

Notice that much of the time we don't even get through a checkout line happily — because we decide beforehand how much time it should take for our line to move. In one activity after another, we become our own self-imposed thief. We do save time, but we rob ourselves of peace.

ACCEPTANCE IS
THE FIRST STEP

Stand naked before a mirror and say, "This is the body I have."

Yuck.

No, "yuck" prevents you from seeing your body honestly.

Yuck. Yuck. Yuck.

That's not helpful.

In all aspects of life, acceptance is the first step toward attitudinal comfort. However, it's impossible to fully accept present circumstances as long as we believe that it "shouldn't" be this way.

I shouldn't have to work under these conditions. I shouldn't have to stop drinking. I shouldn't have to put up with this part of my partner's personality. I shouldn't have to give up certain sports because of my age. I shouldn't have to cut back on how much I spend.

As long as we feel victimized by our own life story, we deny ourselves access to the one part of our mind that could be of real help: our attitude.

We can change an attitude but not until we clearly see its present objective. For example, once we look at our body honestly, if there is something we want to do about our attitude toward it, we are empowered to do so. But if, for example, we think, *I shouldn't weigh this much*, we can't approach the subject in a balanced, practical way. Our attitude is split between two opposing objectives: To lose weight. And to attack ourselves for how much we weigh. One objective relies on strength; the other undermines that strength.

Most people see their pets clearly. If they notice that excess weight is beginning to threaten the health of their pet, they are not filled with instant dislike of the pet. They simply modify what they are feeding it, and they do this with objectivity.

Yet some of these same pet owners may get a little crazy when it comes to their *own* weight. Why? Because their attitude toward themselves is distorted by *It shouldn't be this way*. Possibly this thought is reinforced with *I shouldn't have this metabolism*. Or, *I work such long hours that I should be able to eat what I want as a reward*. Or, *Our culture is wrong to look down on individuals whose weight is not ideal*.

There are no good facts or bad facts. A fact is a fact. I weigh now what I weigh now. My partner has the personality they have. If I am an alcoholic, I am an alcoholic. If circumstances have changed at work, circumstances have changed.

It's a mistake to have a negative or a positive attitude toward a fact.

As we go through the day practicing acceptance of the situation at hand, our attitudes become less conflicted and extreme and eventually begin to resemble peace. Acting from a quiet mind doesn't work miracles, but it does tend to modify our behavior. Our awareness broadens, and we cope more intelligently. Of course, there will be times when we regress a bit, but it will be much easier to return to peace, because we have truly experienced it.

Once we experience some degree of peace, we are motivated to live in a way that protects that peace. We eat a healthier diet; we don't spend more than we make; we stop saying things that trigger other people's egos.

As counterintuitive as it may seem, full acceptance of even very negative circumstances can lead to increased light-heartedness. And honest acknowledgment of *inner* darkness can open awareness of a still deeper light.

Denying our shadow side actually increases its power over us. When you were a child, perhaps like me you tried to deny that there was a monster under your bed. The more you denied, the more your fear grew. What works is to take a light and actually look under the bed. The same direct approach holds true with conflicted attitudes.

When we accept all parts of ourselves and then make an informed choice about which parts we want to strengthen, we lessen conflict. A split mind is of no use to anyone. Unified attitudes may require effort to attain, yet the effort begins to draw together the scattered parts of ourselves and we feel more real. In fact, we *are* more real.

ON BABBLING

If you're a brook, babbling suits you. *Am I a brook?*

When I find myself jabbering, I ask myself: *What am I afraid of? What is the hole in me, or the conversation, or the relationship that I am trying to fill?* I find this helpful because to look at a hole is to automatically begin filling it.

Then there's the little matter of having to listen to a non-brook babbler. A crowded movie theater comes to mind. If you say something to chatty moviegoers, then you usually have to deal with the negative attitude that comes your way for the rest of the movie.

So, what to do? In my opinion the mistake is to just sit there in conflict. Where there is conflict, there can be no peace or enjoyment. So, I ask myself, *What do I want to do about this?* And I keep asking until I see clearly that I can only be a victim by choice.

If moving is possible, I move. An inferior seat is better than mental turmoil. Sometimes a game will work. I have pretended that I am a famous doctor specializing in autism and these people are talking for the first time. Hearing them is music to my ears. Frankly, that worked for only a short period, but it did show me the power of the mind, because if that were the actual situation, I would indeed be happy, despite the fact that the babbling would be the same.

Then there's the sneaky approach of getting up and telling a manager, or lobbing popcorn, or making surreptitious shushing sounds. But all of those come with potential negative side effects. I speak from experience. It's about this time that I begin hoping there is *someone* who is not on a spiritual path who will stand up and tell them to be quiet.

One person I know told a couple who couldn't stop chattering that he was writing a review of the movie, and he hoped they didn't mind that he was going to quote them. He's a good actor and actually pulled this off.

I am conflicted if I babble. And I am conflicted if I frustratingly endure babble. In fact, conflict itself is mere discordant inner babble. So, we get back to the question *Am I a brook?* Of course I am. We all have a calm, melodious inner brook. The real question is how often we listen to it.

LITTLE CHILDREN

Little children are better human beings than adults.

Having Children

Couples ask themselves, "Should we have a baby?" That's a mistake. A better question is, "Should we have a teenager?"

The baby stage lasts a little over a year. The teen stage lasts a minimum of seven years. And, in reality, the teen *mindset* can begin before the age of thirteen and extend well beyond nineteen. There are even a few thirty- or forty-year-olds who are still teenagers, yet their parents cannot escape being their parents.

Rejecting a child doesn't work. If one wishes to have mental freedom and comfort, rejection of *any* close relative will sabotage both. This does not imply that one has to spend more time, or any time, with every last family member. It simply means that for a mind to be wholly at peace, it must be whole. It must find some way to wrap its mental arms around everyone.

For most couples, having a baby triggers a profound transformation. Just being present at a birth can be like witnessing a miracle. The new mother or father feels, perhaps for the first time, a deep well of unselfishness — so deep, in fact, that they might find themselves praying that they be allowed to take on their child's illness, that if someone must die, let it be them.

That is the initial miracle. It comes up front as a free gift. But now a deep conviction must possess us that we will never allow what we have experienced to fade. Through grace we are given Divine insight. Our heart starts out in the right place. But once the gift is received, it is up to us to cherish it and keep it sacred.

Yet for some couples, the whole baby thing soon becomes tedious, exhausting, even depressing. I am not referring here to postpartum depression, which is generally caused by a dramatic drop in hormones and extreme sleep deprivation, and should be diagnosed and treated. Women who experience it often try to deny its existence and/or feel guilty, which isn't helpful or even true. It is important to accept that this is a condition that is no one's fault and that requires both recognition and understanding. For those who are not suffering from postpartum depression, parental euphoria can rapidly fade. At first the child is interesting, maybe even a source of pride, but gradually it becomes something that must be tolerated. Eventually it is no longer a part of the couple's real life. It is not central to the couple's dreams and pursuits.

A child must be the bedrock of a couple's love for each other. It was born of their love for each other, and there it must remain. That is why it is imperative that they inform themselves of the difficulties they will face and make a pact that they will allow nothing to come between themselves and their child.

Some kids, especially boys, don't sleep through the night for the first three years. And it's shocking to many new parents how often their infant cries, especially given the myth that to be a baby is to have all your needs met.

Little children's ideas of a good time are often at odds with those of most adults. They love repetition. "Peekaboo," if left up to the child, could go on for half an hour or more, and the same bedtime story is requested month after month. A harmonious relationship between parent and child is up to the parent. It is best to let go of adult ideas of what is entertaining, fun, and interesting and instead see the world through the eyes of the child.

Other relationships can also take a beating. Talking to your friends about your baby to the exclusion of all other subjects is mind-numbing and guaranteed to strip conversation of mutual enjoyment. And we're still speaking here only about the baby stage. Still to come is the insane competition that can develop between families about whose child potty trains first, is better looking, has the most talent, is the most popular, scores the highest IQ, gets into the best college, and so on.

Perhaps the most destructive mistake individuals make when deciding whether to have a baby is to factor in the holes in their relationship. Hoping that a baby will foster more closeness, generate commitment, or spice up a relationship that has gone flat places impossible expectations on the child. These motives also set up a sense of defeat when parenthood not only fails to improve things but seems to make them worse.

Negative pressure on a marriage is compounded if one partner has pushed the other into "starting a family." The person who was pressured may look for signs of why they were right to resist and may unconsciously act in ways that make parenthood seem miserable. On the other hand, the individual who did the pressuring will often scrutinize the behavior of their formerly reluctant partner for indications that they are not devoted to their baby.

It's essential to a couple's future peace and happiness that they see in advance that the child, who at times will seem to be the cause of hardships, is completely blameless. The couple must therefore form a pact that they will behold nothing but innocence in their infant, their toddler, their preteen, their teenager, their adult child. Contrary to current thinking, parents who see their children as innocent perceive the personality differences and needs of each of their children more clearly and respond more appropriately.

Having children is not a virtue. Nor is not having children. It is virtuous for two people to be of one mind regarding this life-changing decision. A precious little child coming into a family deserves no less.

ON PRIDE

There is a line that pride should not cross. Loving parents, for instance, find numerous occasions throughout their lives to tell their kids, "I'm so proud of you!" This sentiment comes from a warm heart and warms the heart of the child.

But a line is crossed if children are used as a way for parents to feel pride that their child is superior. This is perhaps an example of the pride found in Proverbs that goeth "before a fall." If we believe we are superior, we *will* eventually fall over the truth of equality. Meanwhile it is a miserable state to be in, ever watchful for slights and always taking offense when no offense is meant.

The choice is either to take pride in others or to allow pride to take you. In one world, you share surrounding fields of surprising beauty with others; in the other, you teeter on the peak of a self-created illusion, and no one is there to share even this.

THOUGHTS

If all minds are joined, shouldn't my angry thoughts about "them" have an effect equal to my blessings? And if our prayers can heal others, wouldn't it follow that our curses could make them sick?

The answer is no. To believe otherwise is a mistake that blocks the insight that nursing a grudge harms only us.

Clearly, if we are in the physical presence of someone, we can usually pick up their attitude toward us, even if unspoken. There are so many physical indicators of how this communication takes place that there is now a separate discipline devoted to examining them. But I would imagine that the way we naturally focus on the specific individuals near us physically also opens us mentally to their mindset.

Some people are obviously better at this than others. I know this because I am the odd man out in our family. Gayle and our two boys are so good at reading thoughts that I have had to change a number of mental habits just to keep my inner jerk from being constantly exposed.

There should be little doubt that there are circumstances where we "pick up" other people's thoughts. Thinking of someone just before they call or text is another common example.

What we do with these thoughts is entirely up to us. There are hundreds of ways to react to a thought. So, if I don't *want* to be the victim of another's attitude, I won't be. That should be obvious.

As we go through the day and some judgmental thought about someone crosses our mind, very seldom does the individual we just thought of think, *Oh, so-and-so just had a bad thought about me.* In my opinion, the reason for this is that the judgment took place within our little, rather than our larger, mind. Inside our rigidly defined and past-based self-image, we deeply believe that our thoughts are private and separate from theirs.

If ego-based thoughts were actually powerful, unpopular presidents would get sick and die, athletic teams would always win home games, and widespread beliefs about a given world catastrophe occurring at a specific time, such as Y2K and 2012, would bring them about.

In a dream at night, the mind divides itself into multiple figures, all of whom can say and do things that surprise us, even though it is our own mind that is telling them what to do and say. The reason is that we believe that all minds in the dream are separate from each other and from ours.

In waking life, our little mind believes just as deeply in private thoughts, thus rendering it exceedingly weak and virtually incapable of causing damage through our grievances and judgments. On that level, attack thoughts harm the mind of the attacker, not the mind of the one being attacked.

On the other hand, if we hold someone in light, we are, in a sense, using another mind altogether. Our peaceful mind functions in a realm quite apart from our little mind. Our peaceful mind is joined to the peace within every individual, because peace is whole — so whole, in fact, that in many scriptures it is a synonym for God.

If we are still and at peace, we can silently speak to the mind of the individual we want to bless, and more often than not it will be felt. Gayle and I have taught this approach to many people whose partners are not open to "talking things out." Repeated inner communications can at times be so powerful that seemingly impossible-to-overcome impasses dissolve.

We need not fear other people's thoughts. We also need not sabotage our happiness by deceiving ourselves that we are punishing a wrongdoer by judging them. However, we do need to bless with our blessed mind, because giving and re-ceiving are one.

On Boredom

Boredom, like any ego attitude, can be looked at as a set of bodily sensations triggered by certain thoughts. This little package of feelings is noticed, and the mind decides to label it "boredom." Another person might take a similar package and label it discouragement, loneliness, a respite from turmoil, or something else. The point is that boredom is not a discrete reality, and for this reason it does not have to be approached as something you must fear or battle.

Boredom is a very interesting package that can be calmly opened and examined. It can even become an object of meditation. If the bored individual chooses not to judge it as unwanted, something to avoid or to flee from, the package contents are far more varied and informative than one would expect.

Boredom is usually thought of as an absence of stimulus. The individual feels encased in dullness and tedium, and the tendency is to overreact. Yet if you closely inspect the components of this particular episode of boredom, you will discover a wise set of instructions.

Once you have had one or two experiences of another reality, the mistake of staying bored becomes more difficult. If you confine your attention to your surroundings and immediate lines of thought, you can definitely feel bored. But when you remember that it's possible to allow the mind to soar, an uplifting breeze begins to blow. Soaring thoughts are very still. Picture your mind taking off on great wings of light and ask not where they are carrying you.

DIFFICULT FRIENDS

Some friends are so exhausting. Especially ones who have to control everything.

Ah, control freaks. We should love them all. I have even heard it said that they, too, are children of God. Easy for God, who doesn't have to deal with their control issues, to assert.

Perhaps you know people who get it in their minds that you should do something, and simply will not let it be. I recently had lunch with a friend who not only told me that my favorite restaurant was "not very good" but also insisted that I take his route to his far better restaurant.

"Do you know where it is?" he asked.

"Yes," I said.

"What road will you take?"

"Orange Grove."

"No," he said. "Take Ina."

"But Ina's in the opposite direction from where I live."

"Take Ina. I've tried it. It's much better."

When I arrived, he wanted to know if I had taken Ina. I lied and said yes.

Control freaks. What happened to these poor souls that they got this way? I've noticed that many of them were not cherished and respected as children and seem to feel loved only when another does what they demand. Some people try taking a very hard line against being controlled, but that can destroy the relationship.

I think it's naive to advise people to "just say no" to their overcontrolling friends. When we end a friendship by being critical, we now have someone out there who perhaps feels abandoned, possibly betrayed, and may remain angry for a very long time. So, we are now going to have to deal with that and have merely traded one problem for another.

Those who say, "Just tell them how you feel," often add, "They need to hear it." But isn't that making the same mistake that overly controlling individuals make? They "honestly" think they know what's best for us and they are "only trying to be helpful."

I don't believe that there's some magic formula for this problem, and certainly there are occasional relationships that become so burdensome that we need to step back for a while. But as we step back physically, it is vital that we step up our silent blessings and hold this friend in light whenever they cross our mind. Otherwise, we become susceptible to guilt and, not inconsequentially, we miss an opportunity to practice mental kindness.

Usually, we understand that an old friend's desire to control is just one part of them, that they have other wonderful qualities, so we accept them as they are. We don't fixate on just one quality. Here again is the Golden Rule, for isn't that the understanding attitude we would want others to have toward us?

THE VIRTUE OF OMISSION

"The sin of omission." Ah, but what of the virtue of omission?

"Don't get me started," people say when someone has just brought up a subject about which they are tempted to rant. Surely we can refrain from feeding other people's egos. And what about bringing up political or religious triggers? Isn't love more present when controversy is omitted? And what about telling someone what another person said about them? We say we are just being their friend to let them know. But doesn't a true friend omit what will only distress and solve nothing?

Omit what will not bring you peace.

Practicing Charity

An act of charity is often equated with giving money to a commendable cause. The motive to do this is often worthy, but it *can* be unworthy. *Inner* charity can have only one motive: love.

Charity as a movement within the heart, a spontaneous act of tenderness and understanding, comes more easily when we are the sole recipient, and it's clearly much more difficult to feel compassion for people we don't like.

In one of our early books Gayle and I tell the story of, because of limited choices, having to rent a car made by a company with which we had had several bad experiences. We were visiting Orcas Island to see if we wanted to move there. The people were nice, the weather was perfect, and the ocean was only a short drive away from the nice house we had rented.

So why weren't we happy?

The answer was that we were judgmental, not of a person but of a car. A car!

One of the first things we had done when we arrived was to go to a small store to stock up on provisions. When we were leaving, a man walked up to us and said, "How do you like your car?" So, we told him about the trouble we were having with it, "but what can you expect when you consider the manufacturer?"

"Oh," he said. "I just bought one."

We tried valiantly to backtrack, but the damage had been done.

We immediately went back to our place and began meditating. Soon the answer was clear. Our judgment of a car had infected our minds. That was the first time that we had seen that judgment is a complete mindset. By judging even an inanimate object, we had hurt not only ourselves but now another person.

Forgiving the car came fairly easily. The car was innocent. After all, it was just a car. Then began the work of inner charity. There was nothing outward we could do for the man we had so obviously depressed. But there was something we could do with our hearts, and that was to bless him. We made the decision that whenever he crossed our minds, we would stop and see him as whole and happy driving along in his innocent car!

One way of practicing charity is to picture the individual who doesn't seem whole — whether depressed, sad, obnoxious, insensitive, cruel, or any of a thousand other perceptions — as what they will eventually become.

Practicing charity acknowledges a purity in the other person that we do not yet see in ourselves. In this way it draws us forward. One way to do this is to picture the individual as if they had already made great spiritual progress. This does two things. It affirms that their progress is as inevitable as yours and mine, and it confirms that this individual will inevitably accept the gift we now offer them. It is both an act of faith in them and an act of faith in the power of charity.

An effective exercise is to take up just one grudge, then examine all the areas of your life that it has seeped into. This can lead to an appalling insight, and most people are unwilling to be that thoroughly honest. They do not like how it makes them feel about themselves, even though we must first admit our weaknesses before we can see our strengths.

You become the guilt you see in others. Just notice in most conversations how often people criticize in others what they themselves do in a different form. We think that criticism distances us from the actions of those we criticize. And perhaps our actions are not identical to theirs, but the censure we feel is internalized and it slowly transforms us.

Correcting a lack of charity can be fairly straightforward. The steps I usually take are first to acknowledge the mistake (that part is essential), then ask myself what I can do differently in the future, and then do what my better nature asks of me in the present: forgive myself, forgive all others; essentially, hold on to nothing that is not love.

Charity, like forgiveness, means to let go, to cease to harbor, to stop chewing on. So, you don't want to endlessly review the mistake, because that is a denial that God was present at the time you or someone else made the mistake. In fact, from the standpoint of absolute Truth, either the mistake took place or God took place. If the mistake is Truth, then God (Oneness, Love, Perfection, Peace) is not true.

To continue to dwell on a mistake is a form of arrogance, not humility, because it means that we think we were so powerful that we thwarted God's will. So, forgiving ourselves is an affirmation of what God is and what God created. Since our mind is connected to all other minds, if we forgive ourselves, that forgiveness will of itself extend to them.

The ego loves to torture itself. Being miserable is one of the ploys it uses to keep us believing that we are separate, that we are small and alone. But God asks us to be happy, to love and feel loved, and, over and over, to sink deeply into the peaceful present.

So, whenever the guilt comes to mind, be charitable. Physically stop, and acting from God, who is your strength, say, "We are still as God created us. To think otherwise is to deny Truth. I refuse to do that. I am determined to see myself and others as God sees us."

On Having a Plan

A plan relies on fantasy. I fantasize about how I want things to go based on past experience. But even the past can be interpreted numerous ways. I go back and forth as to what was or was not a helpful experience. When I become determined to follow through on a plan, I am really saying that I want a future that looks like the past, even though I'm not sure what the past looks like.

It's a mistake to be indecisive, so in that sense having a plan can help reduce fear. However, deciding should include the option of deciding not to decide. Sometimes *not* "doing something about it" has more profound and pleasing effects than doggedly following through.

ON MAKING A PLAN

The world doesn't work.

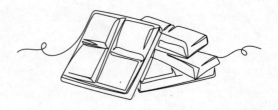

Reset Your Purpose

Chocolate represents a disturbing and unnatural place in Gayle's and my life. So, it probably comes as no surprise that the reminder I use to set my purpose for the day is a nine-inch-tall, twenty-two-ounce House of Brussels can of "gourmet drinking chocolate." (But it's "maximum dark," so it's very healthy.)

I place the can (black with brass accents) so I would have to trip over it to get out of the bedroom without stopping. This reminds me, before I do anything else, to set my purpose for the day.

Yet I know from experience that at some point in the day I will get off track. I will get caught up in the world and make an external goal (like insisting that I be heard) more important than my state of mind. Thus, I need a way to restart the day.

Here again chocolate plays a role. I carry a few chocolates to be used for one purpose only. I got this idea from my father-in-law, who had low blood sugar and had been told by his doctor to carry small candies to eat if he became faint.

My method is admittedly a little sick. First, I acknowledge that I am no longer focused on my purpose. Then I stand or sit down and take out a chocolate and say, "As I feed my body, I feed my mind. With this chocolate I start the day over." As I chew and swallow, I reset my purpose. It's sort of a mini-Communion, with chocolate as the Eucharist, although I would never say that because it would be sacrilegious.

Is There a Way
to Enjoy This?

"A chore and a bore." Can a chore, which is something we *have* to do, be turned into something we want to do? Much has been written on this subject, especially because most people think of their jobs as nothing but a series of chores. Housework is also often viewed as a grind.

The mistake we make is to stubbornly refuse to challenge our entrenched negative attitudes. "Do you know what I can't stand?" is an underlying theme so prevalent in most conversations that people often identify themselves and others primarily by their dislikes. In my opinion, except when it is bitter, there isn't a great deal of harm in this, but it does indicate our commitment to complaining. We are actually proud of what we don't like.

One way to correct this is to look closely at the mundane task in question and ask yourself if there is a way to enjoy it. (Notice the resistance to doing just that much.) For of course there is a way. There are a hundred ways. But how much do we really want to change our attitude? How much of our imagination and creativity are we willing to use?

THE HEART OF EVERY
RELIGIOUS PRACTICE IS
PERSISTENCE

I was catching up on old times with a friend recently and told him that Gayle and I had decided to commit to our church by attending services regularly. He said, "I go from time to time, but if I go too often, I don't feel as close to God."

Having attended various kinds of services, I knew well what he was talking about. Even when Gayle and I ourselves have been ministers at a couple of different churches, it's been surprising how little God is present in most church activities.

In the mid-1970s Gayle and I began studying *A Course in Miracles*. In the late seventies, Gayle and I started a grief support group in Santa Fe, New Mexico, which soon morphed into The Dispensable Church, a legal religion based on the *Course*. It was an all-volunteer organization, and when we passed the plate, you could either put money in or take it out, depending on your need.

This practice spread to other churches in Santa Fe, and unfortunately, we began getting angry calls from ministers. They also didn't like our rule that spiritual concepts were never to be taught to children in our Sunday school. We just wanted kids to be kids, since most of them were already practicing what we adults were striving to relearn. So, we hired the best children's entertainers we could find and made having fun the only goal.

Some churches thought the kids were having entirely too much fun and that having fun was simply a ploy to steal parents from their congregations and turn them into Dispensapalians. (When asked their religion, congregants who didn't call themselves Dispensapalians would answer "I'm Hughish." But we never got a call from a rabbi.)

It's a mistake to make a church the object of devotion. For a building and its name to be one's ultimate destination point is as irrational as permanently camping out around a highway sign because it points to a "city upon a hill." The true function of a church is to make itself dispensable. A house of worship, no matter what the religion, should merely point the way.

As people of faith, we seek the experience of the Divine. By that I mean a state in which the light of God is more dominant within our mind than the daily grind. The body is not perfectible. Daily events are not controllable. Death is inevitable. Yet it is possible for the tragedy of human life to fade as the peace of God becomes our preoccupation.

An enlightened mind is one that focuses more on the sweet stillness of the Divine than on what is not going our way.

Every instant we are at peace, we are enlightened. Thus, enlightenment occurs only in the present.

How is this accomplished? Simply by wanting God more than the world, by wanting God "with all thy heart," as Jesus says in Matthew.

While this principle is simple and straightforward, it is difficult to practice. Thus, the heart of every religious practice is persistence.

Shut Up, Be Clear

If partners would simply keep their mouths shut, they would prevent two-thirds of all relationship problems. (That drops to less than half if there's an eye roll.)

Words usually cause more problems than they solve. Even though words can facilitate closeness, more often than not, they increase separation. Yet our culture places a high priority on "talking it out," and today's psychology encourages a preoccupation with words by overemphasizing "processing" and "being honest."

Just how ineffective the words-first approach is can be seen in the frequency with which most partners have the same dead-end arguments year after year. No matter the triggering issue, the disagreement usually deteriorates into all-too-familiar verbal exchanges. Their desire for closeness and friendship is lost in a destructive game of medicine ball in which guilt is tossed back and forth.

The couple believes that they are engaged in a vital battle of words (or the withholding of words). At the time, nothing seems more critical than winning. Thus, words have for the moment become more important than the relationship. And that moment can have effects extending deep into the couple's future.

Even in interactions on TV between people who get paid to talk, an increase in mutual understanding is rarely the outcome. You would think that if any group could achieve a positive outcome from talking, it would be professional talkers. And yet, when two or more authorities present opposing views, no matter how long they talk, they don't change each other's minds in even minor ways. Just listening to these exchanges is separating.

Words alone don't heal rifts, but love-imbued intention often can. In practical terms this means that we must be acutely aware of the impulse to open our mouths the moment we sense discord. Our ego — the seat of separation — dwells in the sentence layer of the mind. The ego is never still. It chatters and whines and talks endlessly to itself about guilt. Therefore, to just start spewing words when we find that we are at odds with our partner will make matters worse.

We may think we have talked sense or proved our point, and our partner may appear to have come to their senses, but we soon discover there was no increase in love.

Thirty years of relationship counseling have taught Gayle and me that one partner can do it the right way, yet the other partner can take it the wrong way. Still, all we can do is our part. Doing our part — and continuing to do it regardless of outward results — begins to make us whole. And it increases the chance that areas of separation within the relationship will begin to heal.

The best approach is, first, shut up; and, second, become clear. We must take the time to see that we *want* our words to promote closeness. If what we truly desire is for our partner to feel safe around us, to trust us, to feel close, to feel comfortable, this intention will bypass the sentence layer of the mind and plug us into the part of ourselves that is capable of oneness. Once this is accomplished, we automatically communicate in more appropriate ways, which may or may not be with words.

ACCEPTANCE IS YOUR GOAL

As Gayle and I were wrapping up a three-day workshop on relationships, an elderly gentleman stood up in the back of the room, pointed out that he had been married much longer than we had, and said, "Here's all you really need to know. The key to a happy marriage is to say, 'Yes, dear.'"

He was right, because there are no perfectly compatible couples. In fact, as individuals, any two people are different in every respect, even if only in minor ways. They are completely incompatible. Fortunately, in addition to self-images, we also have a spiritual component, and on that level, we are the same.

It's nice to have areas of common interest with your partner, but it isn't necessary. It's also nice if your partner is rich and generous, but it isn't necessary. If two people do not share the same religious beliefs, political opinions, ethnic influences, or tastes in sports and music, or do not agree on whether to eat meat or on whether to choose books over TV, or all of the above, it is still possible for them to form a deep and lasting bond. We have never seen a "deal breaker" that one or more couples had not overcome.

It is no truer that the happiest couples are those whose personalities "match up" than it is that couples who look alike have a much better chance of success. The determining factor is not differences or similarities but rather the degree to which two people accept each other as they are. Those who have surrendered their desire to change their partner can relax. They have the partner they have, and they no longer need to try to perfect that person or look for someone else who is a little different.

Clearly there are extreme cases in which one's partner is deeply destructive, and staying with that person is not a healthy option. But it's surprising how few relationships actually fall into that category. Most couples merely have different versions of the same problems, even though they usually think theirs are unique. We all believe we are singularly tortured.

Acceptance allows vision to move past the facade of ego characteristics to behold something much nicer, much more reliable, much more beautiful. Set acceptance as your goal, and although it may take a while, your partner will gradually transform before your eyes.

A Consistent and Unified Mind

You can have consistency of mind or consistency of action, but you can't have both. *Treat others as you would have them treat you* is a consistent and all-inclusive state of mind. If, however, I say that I like it when strangers smile and speak, although my actions would be consistent if I did the same to everyone I encountered, I would not be mentally consistent. Some people are made uncomfortable by such overtures.

We must be aware of how the individual *receives* what we do or don't do. If each person is noticed and seen as they are at the moment, we are in a position to love them as we love ourselves.

The person who merely acts out a set of rules, spiritual sounding though they may seem, can at times be insensitive, even cruel. Whereas those who practice a consistent and unified mind see others from the inside out.

Patience Is Faith

The ego finds patience a useful tool. It bides its time until it senses a better time to strike. True patience is the decision to do no harm. The ego always places a time limit on patience. Real patience is the permanent decision to be kind. It consults no internal clock.

Patience is faith. It is gentle surrender. It is the sweet conviction: *I am loved.*

Just Do Your Part

We knew a woman who made an exhaustive list of every possession she had and designated which of her five children was to receive each item. She tried to be completely fair, but she knew that no matter what she did, some decisions were bound to be controversial.

She told us that there would probably be some anger directed at her, but what she hoped to avoid was strife between her kids. In the codicil to her will, she also expressed her deep desire that all grievances be directed at her, and that her children try not to generate any hard feelings toward each other.

After her death, her plan did not go as smoothly as she had hoped, but no entrenched dislike developed between the siblings.

Several years ago, a beloved member of my family died. It was not an unexpected death. Not even an untimely death, considering her age and health. And it would not have been a difficult death if it hadn't been for how family members began treating each other.

Deep ruptures in relationships occur so frequently when a loved one is at the end of life — especially if that individual has money and possessions to be distributed — that it's surprising I was caught off guard when it happened in my own family.

In the months leading up to this relative's death, Gayle and I talked about how it would be important not to become part of the soap opera that was likely to ensue once she died. But when her health took a sudden downward turn, I was not prepared for how quickly the drama began.

The issues that suddenly cropped up rapidly undermined family and friends' desires to protect the mental peace of the one who was dying. Egos mushroomed and sanity withered away. Suddenly everyone who wanted some childhood void filled or old wound healed tried to get the dying person to say or do things that would reverse a lifetime of perceived slights. But the individual still had enough strength to resist changing, and friends and family began turning on each other.

The mistake I made seemed innocent enough. I advocated for this person's right to be left alone. But no one was interested in my suggestions, and my efforts not only didn't improve the situation but seemed to make things worse.

By taking a stand, I had simply become another character in this dark narrative. Finally, I came to my senses and decided to stop participating. Instead, Gayle and I spent a lot of time just holding the relative in light. This did not lessen the emotional storm swirling around her, but it did bring a measure of peace to us and, hopefully, touched the heart of my relative.

Death is the ego's centerpiece, its most powerful symbol of separation. Nothing mobilizes action and triggers emotion like death or the prospect of death. And yet to want something from another person instantly makes us unhappy. The moment the thought enters our mind — whether we act on it or not — that someone needs to cooperate or change, peace becomes impossible. Even if the desire is to obtain some sign of love or loyalty from a spouse, child, parent, grandparent, or friend, we still make ourselves small and needy within our own perception.

If this is kept in mind, the effects of death and dying can be utilized to make substantial spiritual progress. For example, instead of trying to get a dying parent to admit mistakes or finally say the words of love we have never heard, we can concentrate on identifying the parts of our past that we continue bringing into the present.

Being physically near a parent or other relative who is dying can trigger old grievances, even if no words are spoken. But this can be a helpful phenomenon if our desire is increased freedom from the past.

Death is the ego's visual evidence that eternal life is not real and that oneness does not exist. But despite this evidence, the fact remains that the Truth is true. And this can be experienced under any circumstances. Even as we grieve a loved one's death and wrestle with the inequities that may exist within the situation, it is possible to feel peace and quietly to extend it.

All we can ever do is our part. And that is sufficient. In the midst of death and dying, we can be understanding of those who are being disruptive. We can be a friend to anyone being criticized for the way they grieve, be it too demonstrative or not demonstrative enough. We can be accepting of those who suddenly become petty and greedy. We can be a true member of the family, and we can do so without drawing any attention to our approach.

ALL THINGS I DO
I WILL DO IN PEACE

The sentence layer of the mind is continually deciding, but if you take a closer look, you see that all it is doing is second-guessing. Something deeper is deciding.

Notice that you usually don't get out of bed at the precise moment you decide to. Sometimes you decide to get up but linger; sometimes you decide to linger but immediately get up; sometimes you get up without consciously deciding anything. And every tiny activity from that point on proceeds in a similar fashion. The sentence layer of the mind decides to do something, but the body does not follow its directions precisely or even at all.

And yet something is deciding. And it is obviously contained within the mind. The mistake we make is in not focusing on which part of our mind is deciding at any given moment. We vacillate between our stillness and our confusion and generally have no idea what kind of day we will end up having.

In my opinion, the key is to focus on the *quality* of the mind itself. What kind of mind do we want making our decisions? Do we want a calm mind or a conflicted mind?

When the mother of a friend of ours used to take her dog for his morning walk, she would stop and chat with a couple who walked their dog, Pearl, at the same time. She liked the couple, and the two dogs got along just fine. One morning, after several years of these encounters, she was surprised to see the couple walking a different dog.

"Where's Pearl?" she asked.

The last time she had seen them, Pearl had seemed her usual exuberant self.

"We had to put her down," the husband said.

"Oh, how awful! What happened?"

"We loved her so much," the wife said. "We were constantly tortured by the thought that she could get sick and die. As you know, she was a Shih Tzu, and Shih Tzus have a lifespan of ten to fourteen years."

"How old was she?"

"She was already nine." They both nodded at the same time as if this all made perfect sense.

They loved Pearl, but they chose the fearful part of their minds as their source for decisions about her.

As little kids we are up for almost anything, except brushing our teeth or finishing our steamed beets. Then things begin to happen, painful things, like a never-ending filling by an insensitive dentist, the mysterious disappearance of our squeaking, thumping gerbil, a road trip with no time to see "The Thing," and visiting Grandpa, who can't resist pinching our cheeks.

Thus, the size of a world once brimming with unlimited options begins to shrink, or more accurately, our mind begins to shrink, as buoyancy and pure enjoyment are squeezed out. By the time we are "mature," we can't even enjoy most meals or movies, because our mind now scrutinizes every string bean or twist of a plot to see what is lacking, and there is always something lacking.

We must learn to question the usual question, which is *Do I think I will like meeting this person, running this errand, going on this trip, attending this party, doing this favor?* Since there is seldom any way to know whether we will like it or not, we should look at our state of mind, rather than the question. Within the present, we can always discern the option that holds the most peace by pausing long enough to engage our inner stillness.

In fact, we can set a peaceful purpose for the entire day and follow it. As we practice this, our decisions become more comfortable. *All that I do I will do in peace*, we repeat to ourselves. Thus, decisions begin to lose their aura of big or small, pivotal or inconsequential, fearful or tedious, and we start to experience mental ease. Our decisions are still continual, but now they flow from calm waters.

ONENESS

Outward defensiveness is usually obvious, even though it is often masked as self-respect. But to those who hear it, the individual is clearly being defensive. Circumstances may seem to justify it or not, but what is often overlooked is the common impulse underlying the desire to be defensive, which is to establish our autonomy.

We believe that our mind is private property and that our thoughts are the one thing we can keep to ourselves. This part of us, held separate from all other minds, is our worldly identity, the one thing we keep regardless of what changes around us. And so, believing that our separateness has great value, we fight against anything that seems to threaten it.

The problem this mistake creates is enormous. Oneness is the only thing that makes the world tolerable. To choose loneliness over acceptance assures that we will have no lasting happiness or peace and never experience a sweet, pervasive love. If only we could realize how important each person is to the recognition of all that we are in truth.

Either we are all connected or connection is limited, temporary, and illusory. To be defensive we must make ourselves so small that we block all understanding that God, the limitless, is our source and our home.

Mental defensiveness is far more pervasive than outward expressions of it. A surprisingly large percentage of our memories, fantasies, projections, and "idle thoughts" are defensive in nature. Once we recognize it, to continue pursuing a defensive line of thought perpetuates an attack on ourselves. The defensive thought appears to shift blame to someone else, but in truth it merely feeds our ego, which grows in loneliness.

When you feel an urge to be defensive, know that you have merely identified with your belief that you are separate, and that is not the direction you want to go. Decide instead to walk in grandeur. Decide to be as large and whole and happy as you were created. Practice this and then watch as home becomes more all-embracing and beautiful.

Turning the Mind
to Peace

To make our state of mind more important than what we are doing is to walk a spiritual path. That's pretty basic. But it all becomes a little more complicated when we recognize how often we fall short of our goal and so turn to one or more spiritual methods, religions, systems, and teachings to help us progress more rapidly. Once we discover that there is no end to possible approaches, even within the same path, we can get entangled in questions of form over substance.

If you, like me, believe that consistency is the measure of spiritual progress, you can now relax. Because if you have doubts about your personal strength, determination, or ability to walk your talk, without ever meeting you, I can assure you that your capacity to be consistent is more than adequate.

Increasingly our spiritual journey is to recognize the importance of our mental state, but what is the nature of the state we seek? It has been described in countless ways. Love, acceptance, joy, stillness, charity, understanding, oneness, selflessness, and happiness are only a few. Note that all of them are forms of connection. On a spiritual path we want our connected mind more than our judgmental mind. And we want this connected mind to expand throughout our experience until it encompasses everyone.

The state of mind we have chosen to learn can be called anything one wishes, but it must be understood as profound, complete, all-encompassing, and allowing for no exceptions. I personally use and deeply love the word *God*. Often, I simply repeat that word as my sole meditation. So, the mindset I ultimately seek is *the peace of God*. When I think of Truth, of what is ultimately true here and now, it is that God is love, that God is peace. I have come to believe that what prevents me from experiencing the peace of God at any given moment is my focus on something quite different. In short, I have become preoccupied with some random incident of worldly chaos. And each day provides a lot of those.

I recognize that the word *God* can be considered divisive; we live in a world of division, so this should not be surprising. After all, religions fight against each other and/or insist that they are the one true faith and that all others are heresy. And having faith in God and religion does not automatically make an individual peaceful or loving, which means that even those who do not believe in God or religion and consider themselves atheists can be more loving and spiritual than those who do if they practice kindness, forgiveness, and love.

It is my choice alone to focus on whatever "the problem" is. And the problem can be, and often is, not an outward circumstance but a memory, a worry, or an emotion. Yet once I choose to lose my focus, it can stay lost for many minutes, hours, sometimes days. A part of me always becomes aware of what I am doing, but I tell myself that I just don't have time to turn to God's peace right now. Or I will make some half-hearted spiritual effort, but my mind is still giving priority to the problem.

As I said earlier, awakening is a matter of persistence and starting over. Awakening is also a present, not a future, state. Anyone who is peaceful, happy, and loving in the present is awake in the present. To reach a prolonged awakened state requires a speedup of focus corrections. It must become like breathing. The ego presents; the peaceful mind says, *No, thanks.* The ego presents; the peaceful mind says, *No, thanks.* And over and over again.

I believe this is possible, and Gayle and I know one person who we know for certain attained just such a state. But he got there through many years of persistence and starting over.

It all boils down to, first, recognizing the signs that we are getting caught up in the world and, second, immediately turning the mind to peace. And we do this without condemnation of ourselves or anyone else.

PROTECTING YOUR PEACE

Once you feel peace born within you, are you vigilant in protecting it? Or do you mistakenly choose your destination points out of mere habit or convenience? Just to save a few minutes, a few pennies, or the difficulty of saying no, we often frequent stores, banks, offices, restaurants, or gatherings that we know from experience will probably upset us in some way. We *do* complete the undertaking, but as we leave, does peace still comfort and guide us?

Protect your peace the way a mother bird protects her hatchlings. She builds a strong nest below, and above, she unfolds her feathers and her wings. She shelters, sometimes even with her life, what she cherishes most.

WHEN RELATIONSHIPS COLLAPSE

Divorce is usually far more disturbing than anticipated. Even grown children are often profoundly affected when they see their parents turn against each other. Many couples believe they can divorce lovingly and peacefully, but few pull this off, because almost no divorce is actually mutual.

Hundreds of books have been written on divorce, and judging by the effects they have on the reader, they tend to promote ego enhancement rather than to heal differences. Most therapists affect couples in a similar way. The central message of our time is "You first have to take care of yourself." But what is *yourself*?

If ever there is a time when anger seems justified, it is when one is betrayed, yet unless the individual being abandoned can find a way to forgive the one they thought was their best friend and life partner, they may carry emptiness, hopelessness, and bitterness in their heart for a very long time. They will also take this into any new relationship and will tend to see their new potential partner through this very sad lens.

Words such as the ones I write here are so inadequate. Divorce can be as devastating as the sudden death of a loved one. And added to the loss is rejection. Overt efforts are often made to regain the affection of the one who is leaving or has left, and these efforts frequently deepen the rift and do further damage to the sense of self-worth of the one making them.

There is also the misery of those who are forced to initiate a divorce, for there are certainly cases when this is necessary. There are feelings of guilt, the shock of former friends and family members suddenly turning against you, and deep doubts as to whether you did everything you could to save the marriage.

Because of the diversity of circumstances under which it can take place, it is simplistic to say that divorce is a mistake, but it is a tragedy with potential long-term consequences and should be avoided if at all possible. Although some of these have been touched on in other parts of this book (and our book *I Will Never Leave You* has many more), Gayle and I have found at least four guidelines that have been helpful to individuals and couples we have counseled whose relationships were on the verge of collapse.

1. Take all pressure off your partner. Make no demands, ask no probing questions, and make no statements that call for a loving response (such as saying, "I love you," because that calls for your partner to answer in kind, and that is pressure). No pressure is the hardest rule to follow. But it is by far the most powerful. When you suddenly take off all

pressure (don't announce it; just do it), your partner often has a very interesting reaction: you become much more interesting in their eyes.

2. As often as you want, silently talk to your partner through your heart. This wordless communication bypasses their defensiveness. Say anything, anything at all, that is on your mind. If setting up chairs helps, do this. But if you picture your partner facing you, be certain to get out of your chair, take a moment to become your partner, and answer back. Keep switching chairs back and forth until you feel at least some increase in insight and understanding.

3. Every time you catch yourself thinking about something that makes you unhappy, write down a few words on a strip of paper, just enough to identify the specific thought. Your ego has a limited number of thoughts to torture you about this tragic circumstance, maybe only ten or twenty. Put each of these strips in a ziplock bag. Keep adding to this as new thoughts arise. These are thoughts of specific events, memories of conversations, rehearsed future conversations, questions about what will happen to you or the children — any thought that keeps torturing you. Now here's the rule: When you discover that you are thinking along one of these lines of thought, you can continue doing so for as long as you want, but first you have to take that thought out

of the bag and hold the strip of paper in your hand. When you have thought about that subject for as long as you want, put the strip back into the bag. This is an extremely powerful exercise for eliminating misery, because it demonstrates that you alone decide what to do with your mind. I know one case in which it prevented a suicide.

4. Recognize that your partner is now a part of your mind. For your own mental health and comfort, you want to heal this part. So, you might hold this person in light whenever they come to mind. Or see a Divine figure standing behind them and watch as this One steps inside them. Or picture how your partner will eventually be once they progress far beyond where they are now spiritually. Say to yourself, *Do I want to be right or be peaceful? Do I want to be a victim or be strong? Do I want to hate or forgive? The power to decide is mine.*

Forgiveness, the most powerful approach in dealing with a finalized divorce, is also the one that gives the couple the best chance of healing their failing relationship. Whether this is the outcome or not, trust that your own peace of mind, about the present or concerning the future, is an attainable goal.

Living *and* Dying

As I write this, my dad is turning ninety-nine. For some time now, he has been under hospice care within his own home, where he prefers to stay. He gently declines any benefit that might come from a hospital visit.

What I find remarkable about this stage of his life is that although his body is swiftly disintegrating (his teeth are falling out, his hearing is almost gone, his eyesight is bad and getting worse, his skin tears at the slightest touch, he has little remaining ability to recall nouns, he has to wear diapers, and he spends his day either in a wheelchair or in bed), he is nevertheless in good spirits most of the time. In fact, he even jokes about what is happening to his body.

"How are you feeling, Dad?"

"Not as good as when I was ninety-six."

"Are you still enjoying life?"

"Well, I'm down to just one girlfriend."

My dad still has the same basic lightheartedness he has had all his life. Here is a man who was bigger, stronger, and better looking than most, a good athlete, a man who loved adventure, enjoyed excellent health, and was always active.

Each of these things, as well as every one of his friends, has been taken from him. All he has left is the lightheartedness. And this, quite frankly, has come as a shock to me. I had always assumed that *of course* he was happy; he had everything.

Clearly, I was wrong.

From what he has told me, the way my dad achieved release from the physical tragedy of age and accident is fairly straightforward. After several bouts debating with himself over whether he wanted to die or to live until he was one hundred, he realized that he had no real control over that, and that he wanted no control. He came to be at peace with both living *and* dying.

In other words, my dad took himself off the battlefield. He bypassed the conflict over whether to live or die and leaned back into his life as it was. This allowed his basic happiness to return, and now he is neither waiting for the inevitable nor fighting to stave it off.

What did my father do to reach this place of balance? I believe there are steps he took that the rest of us might find helpful.

If we begin with the assumption that the function of the mind is not to serve the body but rather it is the body's function to serve the mind, then we will do whatever allows our body to become less of a preoccupation.

This simple rule covers most of the decisions that come up regarding the body: What to eat. How to exercise. Whether to get the operation. How much to discuss our physical problems with others. Whether to complain. (No one in our family has ever heard our father complain.)

We will of necessity orient almost any category of human activity — finances, relationships, employment, parenting — toward either the body or the mind. We have little control over external outcomes, but we do have a choice about what to emphasize mentally.

As our mental state becomes more interesting to us than our physical state, a new option opens up. Now we can base each decision on how it will affect our mind. This inevitably leads to the insight that the mind is self-contained. It exists in and of itself. And it is connected to other minds. And to Truth.

As best you can and only within the moment at hand, trust your mind. Resign as its instructor. Resign as its judge and jury. Make a leap of faith and let your mind be free. It already knows the way home. Make this leap of faith and it will take you there. I know this is possible because I am witnessing my dad do just that.

Two Views of the World

A body is the ego seen. That should be fairly obvious. Apparently, what is not obvious is that all parts of our ego are just as much "us" as our ears and toes.

We identify ourselves with our physical characteristics, even though these change, sometimes quite dramatically, through diet, accident, disease, plastic surgery, and unremittingly through age. Yet when it comes to our thoughts, we believe that we can choose which ones to take responsibility for and which ones to deny responsibility for, because of "nature and nurture."

If we put on a few pounds, we can choose to do something about it or choose not to. But we don't deny ownership of the weight. If we did, we would have no chance of assessing the problem and deciding what to do.

It seems self-apparent that a problem can't be solved until we admit that it is a problem. Our deeper ego thoughts are not a pretty sight, and they continue asserting themselves until fully acknowledged. The destructive patterns of an unaware person, or of a person in denial, are so persistent that often they are taken to the grave. But individuals who decide to be honest with themselves can change even chronic patterns.

The acknowledgment process is similar to admitting, as I have had to do, that I am not a good driver, not a good dieter, not a good manager of money, and not good at remembering appointments. Having acknowledged these things, I am more vigilant when I drive, I weigh in daily, I defer to Gayle on all matters of money, and I set things out to remind myself of appointments.

The essential point is that I will probably never be a good driver and so forth. Therefore, vigilance in those areas is vital. In a broader sense, my ego is already formed, and *it will never improve*. My function is to acknowledge what my ego is up to *now* (say it out loud, if need be) and see that what it tells me I want is my responsibility, it is coming from me, and it presents me with a choice. Having owned up to my ego thoughts, I am now in a position to decide with strength and determination that I will act from my spiritual instincts instead.

Today, many teachings and systems recommend that we distance ourselves from the darkness within us. Growing up a Christian Scientist, I was taught to "deny," quite specifically and forcefully, the negative thoughts of what Mary Baker Eddy called "mortal mind," her term for the ego. Given my experiences practicing this, I do not believe that it is a good mental habit to cultivate, and it has taken me many years to reverse the effects of it.

Some modern teachings are more indirect. Perhaps there is an overemphasis on "high self-esteem," or "affirmative prayer," or "creative visualization," or "the law of attraction." The subtext of many — but not all — of these teachings is that "good" thinking should be increased and "bad" thinking decreased. All too often the effect is that their students tend to turn against their own negative thoughts and distance themselves from their inner darkness.

This may be an adequate approach if you have a very mild ego, coupled with a deep awareness of your spiritual self. Gandhi is an example of someone who could deny his ego impulses with good effect. But most people have at least a few inner demons, and a larger percentage than is perhaps obvious have egos grounded in hate.

Many think that because they are consciously walking a spiritual path, they have thereby weakened their ego. But they actually become more destructive if they start interpreting ego impulses as harmless (*Oh, that's just ego; I don't have to confront that*) or, even worse, begin responding to these thoughts as spiritual guidance. Simply because they *want* to do something, they assume that the urge they feel must be coming from their inner wisdom or, worse, from God, simply because they recognize that they are on a spiritual journey.

It is definitely possible to use spiritual concepts to justify destructive behavior. The ego offers us spiritual-sounding guidance and profound episodes of what can feel like peace. To distinguish these from true guidance and peace, we have to look honestly at the effect we are having on other people, especially our loved ones. If we are truly at peace, we do no harm; we cause no separation; we disseminate no misery; we judge no one.

There are two views of the world. One view offers a false sense of innocence and of personal power over others through grievances and guilt. The other view is aware of love's absence and chooses to be the love that is lacking.

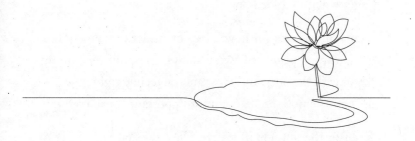

Identifying with Peace Rather Than Emotion

The ego part of us loves to obsess over our emotions. The emotions themselves are not a mistake — it is impossible not to have them — but the importance we are now giving them is mistaken, especially since the triggering thought behind a feeling is often overlooked or dismissed.

When our dog Mousse was dying, the same act, seeking out rugs to pee on, that used to make me angry when she was younger now evoked a tearful sadness, because I knew she was incontinent and that it distressed her to pee inside.

Being aware of the *idea* that dogs with Cushing's disease often did this generated a different emotion. When she was younger and supposedly housebroken, I didn't look for the thought that was making me angry. Instead, I identified with my anger, and although I never struck her, I *became* my anger when I scolded her.

Many interviews with winners of athletic competitions, game shows, pageants, award shows, and political contests begin with the question "How are you feeling right now?" — as if one's emotions are the most important consideration.

Even in therapy, emotions are often the central subject of discussion, and changing the client's prevailing emotion the central goal. To our ego, our transient feelings are our deepest self. Yet within our spiritual core, a reliable peace is the governing emotion.

Most emotions are distractions that don't merit the attention we are programmed to give them. Yes, we must be aware of them so that we don't get caught up in an objective that leads away from what makes us happy and kind. But we don't have to battle them as if they were an opposing and dangerous power.

In fact, since emotions are basically illusory, awareness alone will often disperse them. As I suggest later in dealing with fear and infatuation, it can be helpful to sit and simply look quietly at an emotion and see how it begins to change within minutes, if not seconds.

Or leave the emotion in place but add peace to it. Notice that there is another part of you that is always still and calm. Decide to be peacefully anxious, peacefully sad, peacefully jealous, and the like. When you choose not to honor the emotion, it is detached from its source of power, which is mental focus.

Naturally there are extreme circumstances such as a divorce, death, and illness that continue to trigger a specific kind of intense emotion, and the process must be repeated often. And this is by no means easy, but it is possible.

We need not be a puppet pulled about by erratic emotions. There is a quietness within us that cannot be disturbed, a place of beauty and safety and strength. Do not be lured by random chaos. Look carefully at the emotion. Go back and find the thought that preceded it. Add peace to what you are feeling. Then identify with the peace instead of the emotion.

There is usually a sort of rattle, an agitation, a kind of noise that accompanies ego emotions. Often even an urgency. But kindness and peace do not so much demand attention as gently lift you into stillness.

The Dry Bones
of Your Past

Rigidity is the dry bones of the past. The mind has already left them behind. But it doesn't know it. Speak to your mind about universes and lifetimes. Tell it stories about timelessness and love. Invite it to wander into thoughts so sacred that you would never speak of them to anyone.

Allowing Peace to Come into Awareness

For those who are in it, the world is all too real. And on more occasions than not, for those on a spiritual path, the world defeats us. For what can seem a very long time, there appears to be little we can do about this. In many ways, discouragement, depression, and even anger begin to feel like normal responses.

What can possibly be done in any substantial way about the eroding effects of this picture of separation, loss, insensitivity, and chaos we face each day? I believe that forgiveness offers us a way forward, and while it doesn't change the world, it can transform the way we react to it; from anger, separation, and judgment, forgiveness allows us to connect with those in the world who have awakened to oneness, peace, and love. And we do this by silently forgiving those we believe are responsible for our pain.

Perhaps after our morning meditation or prayer, we believe that today will be the day we will feel that kind of happiness and peace. Then something happens. Then something else happens. After a while, the possibility of such a day once again seems sadly out of reach.

Most of us have learned the hard way what emotional jeopardy having expectations puts us in. An AA friend recently said, "An expectation is a resentment waiting to happen." There are many other unhelpful emotions that expecting can lead to, such as disappointment and frustration, and of course the despair we have been discussing.

Expectation can extend into any area of life, such as how much we should get done or how interactions with certain individuals, agencies, or stores should go. We expect that by the end of the day we will have something to show for our efforts. This attitude imposes specificity on what accomplishments should be waiting there for us. Yet the events of the day seldom cooperate, and we often feel a familiar disappointment. Even *expecting* that a particular movie or dinner with certain friends will be lots of fun can be hazardous.

These are all external expectations. However, the dangers of *spiritual* expectation are often overlooked. *Today I should feel peace. Today I should look gently on others. Today I should not be anxious. Today I will not let so-and-so at the office push my buttons.*

All these seem like worthy thoughts. And they are, except that a *future* goal has been set, a spiritual benchmark. This enlists the ego as the judge of whether we succeed. There is an important difference between saying *Today I should feel peaceful* and *I will be peaceful now.*

Since the day divides itself into segments through a stream of little beginnings and endings, we can consider what we are doing now as the most important thing we could be doing. It's the most important because it's what we *are* doing. We couldn't be doing something else, because we are not. So, unless we want to stop what we are doing and start a new activity, we had better pay attention to what is possible at this moment.

The ego or sentence layer of our mind wants to think about anything except the instant at hand. The more we enter into the present, the further we distance ourselves from that part of us that generates hopelessness, discouragement, depression, and the like. All these emotions draw their power from comparisons with the past. *I'm not as accepting, happy, engaged, peaceful, and so forth as I have been at other times.* Occasions of "good" states of mind are recalled, and our present attitude is found wanting.

Regardless of the reasons, we often find that we are not as happy as we would like to be. There are two common responses. One is to throw up our hands and turn to food, fantasies, TV, crises, sleep, arguments, rants against people in the news, or any other activity that might change our mood. The other is to begin a grand spiritual quest, to set an unattainable objective, to seek an impossible ideal. Note that these are future dependent. We do make an effort, but because of the size of the task we have set for ourselves, failure is assured.

One of the quickest ways to lessen despondency and orient the mind toward peace is to release expectations and to think small. To take little steps in the present.

Here are a few I have found helpful:

1. Perhaps start the day by saying, *I expect nothing of this day. I release my mind from all plans, goals, and agendas. Starting this instant, I will sink deeply into now.*

2. Or play this little game: *To experience peace, it is only necessary to practice the mental condition that allows peace to come into awareness. My mind is a circular pond or reflecting pool into which God shines. But at the moment it is ruffled. I wipe from my mind all ripples of agitation, the disturbed patches of resentment, the swirls of grievances, the restless desires, the unsettling fears. I calm the lovely pool that is my mind until it is like a still mirror where the peace of God can now be seen as mine.*

3. Or this game: As you know, God can dress up as anyone. Is there, in fact, any person the Divine does not inhabit? Today you are attending a celestial costume party. So now do you see how innocent what just happened was? The deeper meaning was not at all what you first thought, for God would never offer you pain. Turn to God and ask who this person really is.

4. Perhaps say, *I don't know what to do. I have failed as my own guide. Now I turn to You. Be my heart, my will, my mind, my life. Possess me and lead me. I give myself to You completely.*

5. Whenever you find yourself heading in the wrong direction, pause and start over. The direction that the mind is taking now is really all that matters.

6. Ask for help often. Having asked, trust that the One who is with you is now helping you.

7. Trust that each individual is God's chosen home.

8. Forgive other people's egos as you would have them forgive yours.

9. Forgive yourself. The desire to remain guilty comes from your ego.

10. Act from strength and certainty.

11. Don't be arrogant and think that you can't learn God's will.

12. Heal everyone and everything. Heal the world. Salvation depends on you. All God's angels lovingly sustain you in this God-given assignment.

God is peace. God embraces you in peace. God guides you through peace. The hand of peace is on your forehead. Feel it now. Then hear peace speak to you these gentle words: *I love you, and I am with you always.*

No matter what small effort you make, remember to have no expectations about the results. Don't ask yourself, *Did that work?* for this just invites your ego to partner with you on your journey through the day. The ego cannot be a true partner, because it is made up of our desire to remain separate. To truly partner is to relax boundaries and soften walls. It is to open rather than to remain tight. Anyone who approaches peace in humility and with open arms will know peace.

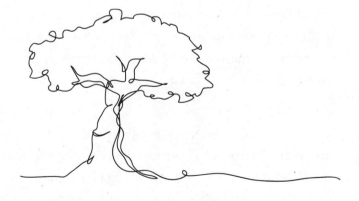

Being a Victim

When speaking of victimhood, I am not referring to illegal acts of cruelty and deprivation. However, while seeking legal justice is both necessary and helpful for the victim(s), as well as for any future victims, it is still important to eventually work to get beyond what was done and to truly heal — to release the spirit from its pain and to walk in the light.

There are clearly times when we feel that we have been unfairly treated. Perhaps we are surprised that someone is upset since we believe that what we did was innocent. Or maybe the ill treatment was unforeseen and seemed to come from out of the blue. Some people are in ongoing relationships, whether with a partner or in a job, in which unfair treatment seems the daily norm.

Unquestionably there are betrayals and injustices, slights and deliberate humiliations. The world abounds with instances of insensitivity and cruelty. But to what degree must this pervasive phenomenon make us feel like a victim for the rest of our lives — to remain living proof of what was done to us?

For me personally, perceiving myself as a victim has been one of the major blocks to experiencing peace. I have thought a lot about this, because long ago I recognized that if I believe that my feelings of mistreatment are beyond my control, I have no chance of recognizing the God-given self within others. How could I see innocence while believing in guilt? How could I experience oneness with my neighbor if my neighbor was my enemy? There were several individuals whom I saw in just that light, plus from-time-to-time encounters with other people who evoked the same self-pity in me. How could I constantly feel the peace and light within me if I felt irreparably damaged by my past?

Feeling unjustly treated, we *will* find ways to attack back. In our eyes our attacks are not only warranted but necessary to maintain our integrity, which is merely another way of saying that we must maintain our ego autonomy. But in order to attack, no matter how we go about doing it, we must take from our perceived abusers their God-given innocence so that innocence will be ours alone.

Thus, being a victim sets up a bitter and incessant circle of defeat. First, we have to choose to feel like a victim. Second, we have to see the one who treated us unjustly as guilty. Third, we have to attack back, whether mentally, overtly, or passive-aggressively, to regain what has been taken from us. Fourth, in order to feel that our attack is innocent, we must take innocence away from our attacker. And fifth, we thereby ensure our own feelings of guilt for having taken innocence away from someone God sees as innocent, so we must start the circle all over again. If it weren't for this other person, we wouldn't have to feel guilty. If it weren't for this other person, we wouldn't be a victim.

There is simply no room for love, acceptance, and the realization of oneness within this cycle of taking innocence in order to have it exclusively, then feeling guilty for partaking in this endless and insane barter.

Once we begin participating in this pattern, it can spread to all areas of our life and become part of our basic identity. Experience any adversity, however mild, and we immediately look to see who is to blame. In our mind there is no doubt that someone is to blame, and we begin filling in the blanks of who it is and why they are guilty.

We also unconsciously set in motion events that we know will "prove" that we are a victim. We ask an innocent question. We make an understandable mistake. We even do things that we tell ourselves are a desire — and that feel like a desire — to be helpful. Yet a part of us knows what the reaction will be. It will inevitably be one that we can interpret as unfair.

This dynamic can start at an early age and continue to metastasize throughout a person's life. This is what happened to me. I was betrayed and taught to betray by parents and stepparents, but I alone decided to carry on the tradition.

There were other lessons that these same individuals taught me that I chose to reject, racial prejudice and homophobia being two of several that come to mind. But I can remember vividly at age nine having the opportunity to reject victimhood and choosing not to, a mistake I continued making most of my life. My mother had left me with a physically abusive father when I was five, but when I finally saw her again, I immediately realized that she did indeed love me, despite having been told for years by my father that she didn't. She tried to hug me, and I turned away from her in anger, a dark decision I continued to live out for decades.

If there are traits, beliefs, and behaviors that we choose not to take from our childhood, then we are responsible for the ones we decide to retain. We are not "wired"; we wire ourselves. And by choosing to hold to the notion that I was a victim, first by being abandoned by my mother and then by being punched and beaten by my father, I began to see the world through this lens, manufacturing injustices everywhere I looked.

Although I know people who have been more controlled by the compulsion to be a victim than I have, still my dynamic is perhaps an extreme example. Yet in studying this problem I have noticed that many people have a version of it and that even a mild case of self-pity is sufficient to block a sustainable peace.

Once victims become enamored with the sensation of being unjustly treated, it can seem to give meaning to their lives. At least they feel *something* deeply. One friend of ours told us how pleasurable it was for her to review all the times in her life she had been unfairly treated. "It is such a wonderful feeling," she said. This insight as to how our ego works to keep us mired in victimhood was extraordinary. Most people will not admit that they love being a victim. And yet that must be seen clearly in order for us to question whether this is a pleasure we truly want.

Victims also have people around them who will listen and sympathize. To be a victim is to be important, to be special, to be the center of attention. It is a kind of power based on the belief in our superior innocence. And when the victim gets revenge, as one who feels misused will often do, their power over others is confirmed. They have turned the tables.

But if we are in fact one with our neighbor, we have merely turned the table on ourselves. Whatever we think we do to others we also do to ourselves. That's the way oneness works. This is very difficult to see and requires exceptional honesty.

But what a miserable way to go through life. Yet many people choose this path to greater or lesser degrees. However, to call them on it makes them feel even more a victim. Confrontation backfires, and anger attacks the attacker.

Since I alone choose the feelings, I experience whatever happens and give it the meaning it has for me; in truth, I can think of myself as unfairly treated only if I choose to. There is no more powerful remedy to victim mentality than to ask oneself, *What do I want?*

Yes, something just happened. And, yes, I can choose to feel sorry for myself. My ego is offering me a gift. *Here, take this and feel innocent and add to your store of justifications for misusing other people. Thus will you add to your potential to be powerful and superior.*

Do I want that gift? I have readily accepted it countless times before. But what did I actually gain? What kind of person did I become as a result? Or do I want to confront this chronic ego habit and put myself in a position to see the goodness in others and to feel peace? When thinking of someone who I believe has mistreated me, I sometimes say, "Until I see innocence in you, I will not see it in myself."

Pain has a threshold, and eventually it dawns on the victim that a new choice must be made. Do they want strength or self-pity? Do they want to be one who judges or one who heals? Do they want to think of themselves as beautiful and good or ugly and malicious? Do they want to love or hate?

Do not answer quickly. Do not underestimate your desire to be a victim. Look at the desire closely and then decide to change. Decide to root out every vestige of this old insanity. Be ruthless about this. Decide to be the kind of person you have always wanted to be.

As Jesus was dying on the cross, he said, "Father, forgive them; for they know not what they do," and with those powerful words, he told us how to live in a world of separation, anger, hatred, war, famine ... all the tragedies that the world has endured since its beginning. Forgiveness is the most powerful protection we have in a world full of chaos and separation, but it is not easy, because our egos believe in judging those who have sinned. It is also easy to get caught up in thinking that if we forgive, we are denying that anything bad happened; of course, that is not accurate or even helpful. Forgiveness is not denial; it is simply the light within us looking upon the world through the eyes of peace, love, and oneness.

Forgiveness does not mean that what happened to us when we were children, teenagers, or adults didn't actually happen, or that we have to somehow find a way to reinterpret it. Rather, it is the willingness to rise above it, and in the process, we become who we truly are. Forgiveness is a gift we give ourselves because we no longer have to see ourselves as damaged or as someone who is justified in their anger due to what they have endured. It is freedom from the past, so when we forgive, we are not giving someone who doesn't deserve to be seen as innocent a gift; we are setting ourselves free to truly be the light that God sees within all of us.

It is impossible to see a sinless world free of hatred, war, and chaos, but it is possible to live peacefully in such a world when we choose forgiveness over judgment and love over hatred. By living this way, we extend the light of God that is within us and all around us, and this, too, has a profound effect on the world ... one that isn't as noticeable as the anger and chaos but calls to that still voice within all of us.

It's OK to Be
Who You Are Now

To one degree or another, all of us grew up under the glare of our parents' expectations. We kid ourselves if we think we did not internalize many of these.

The holiday season usually disproves the notion that we have broken free of our "formative years." This mandatory contact with relatives calls to our history, and often we are surprised to see patterns we thought we were well beyond surface virtually unaltered.

Any family reunion — if we watch our thoughts closely — will remind us of what we have failed to accomplish, at least in the eyes of others. Holidays and anniversaries, even if spent alone, also contain reminders of the impossible ideals our family and culture have taught us. There are singles who commit suicide because of the naive picture they have of the warm, embracing homes other people return to on holidays.

Possibly the most common expectations that surrounded us as we grew up, and that today have become almost institutionalized, concern our so-called unrealized potential:

You can be anything you want. In other words, it's a crying shame you are not something already. Just look at all these four- and five-year-olds running around brimming with confidence. If they only knew they were not something or were not enough of something or were at best just a wee potential.

If you want it bad enough, there's nothing you can't do. Evidently, we don't come with enough "want" to automatically fulfill our potential. But where can we obtain all this wanting that we want so much to want?

Somehow, you have to reach down deep. We have to make ourselves want more. The part of us that wants to want — but whose wanting is evidently insufficient or ineffectual or unengaged — has to change the part of us that's a weak wanter. But weren't we created a weak wanter? So now do we have to re-create ourselves?

The mistake that so many of us make is to believe that we are our external accomplishments. But who can claim that they have accomplished everything expected of them?

The more we yearn to accomplish and the more we value accomplishment for accomplishment's sake, the smaller we seem in our own eyes. It's fine to accomplish. Nothing wrong with doing it right. But merely yearning to accomplish, or making accomplishment our priority, only affirms that we are lacking now.

I believe the answer is to aspire to be common. To be equal. To be human. Oh, how relaxing it is to just be normal! Feeling oneness never diminished anyone.

To be who we already are and to let others be who they already are is an especially important parental value. Kids, like adults, should not be thought of or talked about as if they were a set of outward feats or features.

It's OK to be your core. It's OK to be what you are *now*. It's OK to look inside and see that you are already something. But so many people don't believe they are actually something. They are afraid that if they were to admit to somethingness, they would see their inner nothingness; they would be a "nobody."

Having a plan, a daily plan, a long-term plan, a moment-by-moment plan, does not work against being who we are now. At least it doesn't have to. Planning often removes needless mental fretting. As long as we don't *become* the plan. As long as we remain flexible and open to a better way. Because the world may think we're peachy — or it may not. But one thing is clear: there is no way to gain and maintain the world's approval.

However, there is a way to be happy. It's a reasonable expectation.

WISDOM

Keep it simple.

What Are We
Truly Volunteering?

Everyone is a volunteer. Even someone paid to do a job volunteers the quality of the job. Except in extreme circumstances, each individual is willingly doing *something* right now that they could do differently, or not finish, or not do at all, and all for motives that might be congruent with the activity or at odds with it. We have no control over why people do what they do, but we can and must acknowledge what *we* are volunteering to do.

We think of volunteering as offering services without compensation. Part of friendship is the willingness to help with the little things. Then there is "doing volunteer work," which entails the same willingness but usually on a larger scale.

The operative word is *willingness*. Volunteering out of guilt, reciprocity, self-aggrandizement, the need to "be a caretaker," or, the most unhelpful of all, the desire to sacrifice lacks genuine willingness.

But willingness is an interesting impulse, because although genuine willingness to do the task may be lacking, another kind of willingness has already taken its place. For example, a spouse might volunteer to do a chore, but instead of it being an act of love, it is secretly a sacrifice. Sacrifice is the desire to make another feel guilty. Thus, the exact same chore is completed but with a destructive intent. It is remarkable how many relationships are based on mutual sacrifice instead of mutual love.

The crucial question when volunteering — whether it is to listen to everything that happened at the office, paint the bathroom ceiling "that color," invite second cousins to Thanksgiving dinner, or work at the soup kitchen — is what are we *truly* volunteering? From what part of us does the gesture come? Because the offer — even if carried out perfectly — if not motivated by love, is motivated by some form of separation. The motive, not the gesture, constitutes its value and determines the spiritual consequences.

GIVING FEAR
YOUR FULL ATTENTION

The world (I include myself) is gripped by fear. It is almost suffocating. Few have remained unaffected.

Financial chaos, wars, terrorism, racial injustice, the destruction of the planet, paranoid bigotry, new pandemics ... the list is endless. As our anxiety intensifies, many people also experience an increase in personal health problems. It speeds up the aging process as well. And, clearly, fear takes a devastating toll on relationships.

Because it blocks love, oneness, and peace, fear — no matter its cause — is one of our most destructive emotions. Fear splits, if not shatters, the mind. Where there is fear there is always a mind at war. Thoughts battle each other but never come to a comfortable resolution about anything. That is why worries can never be "resolved." They feed basic fear. They actually make it grow. And it is important to remember that our anxieties, our worries, and our fears have absolutely no effect on the problems of the world; they solve absolutely nothing, but they can have a devastating effect on our lives and relationships.

Coming across rattlesnakes several times a year in the part of Arizona where we live, I understand the practicality of the "fight or flight" response (actually, one should stand still or back away slowly from a coiled rattlesnake, not suddenly flee). But the usual fears that dominate most people's minds are not sudden dangers but are generated by lines of thought on an endless loop.

We keep distressing ourselves with the same internal arguments. Since fear is conflict and our deeper self is love, each fearful thought must be acknowledged if we are to know who we are, what we are, and with what outside ourselves we are joined.

Most people would agree that behind dislike is distrust. But it may be a little harder to acknowledge that behind hate is fear. No one is viewed the same way by everyone, so we must wonder, *Why is this* my *reaction?*

To love one's neighbor as oneself quiets the fearful mind. I have found that to ask, *What about this person am I afraid of?* helps me gain insight into why I personally react to them negatively, and thus it frees me to see more gently and charitably. More love equals less fear.

It is not realistic to assume that we can overcome fear once and for all and reach a conscious state of permanent mental invulnerability. Fear must therefore be dealt with in the present, which is especially important to understand when we are in an ongoing anxiety-producing circumstance such as a life-threatening illness. But even small bouts of fear based on seemingly inconsequential causes are sufficient to throw the mind into turmoil, especially when most of the world is already in a state of anxiety.

It is helpful to focus on the fear at hand. How would you describe it, and where in the body does it seem centered at the moment? Next, any fear is composed of several smaller fears, so to unravel the emotion into its component parts makes it easier to deal with. Take up just one part and look at it closely. You can even put the fear in a chair facing you and carry on a dialogue with it.

Notice that simply by giving the fear your full attention, it begins to dissipate or to change into other kinds of emotions. No fear remains the same when scrutinized. Fear is shadow, and your mind contains light. Never believe that you are making yourself less safe by bringing light to darkness. In fact, it is not uncommon for certain practical steps to come to mind during this process.

If needed, repeat the procedure with each of the other components of the present fear. But if at any time you feel suddenly free of fear, get up and resume your day as usual. When that or another fear returns, repeat the steps.

Now the interesting side effect of dealing with a fear instead of staying stuck in it is that, because all minds are joined, you will notice a lessening of fear in some of the people around you. This indicates that you are perhaps more powerful than you believe. And don't let *that* make you afraid.

A Question

If there's a question whether you should say it, don't say it.

AN APPROACH
TO FORGIVENESS

Our reactions to another's personality are entirely our responsibility. Judgments are not justified. They must be owned. It is therefore understandable why many people on a spiritual path turn to forgiveness for relief. And forgiveness is indeed the most efficient and powerful approach.

However, in the way it is usually practiced, forgiveness often bears little fruit. For example, many individuals eventually conclude that it is simply impossible to forgive their partner. Naturally this also can be true of primary relationships with individuals who are not loved ones, especially those living under the same roof, or people with whom we must interact daily. But perhaps romantic relationships provide the best example of how failure to forgive works, because over the months and years grievances accumulate and reach a point where now almost anything the partner does is irritating.

These "issues" may be dealt with one at a time — sometimes they may even be resolved — but notice that new ones, equally disturbing, merely take their place.

People tell their friends about the latest outrage, yet friends can often see that the complaint is just part of an old pattern. (By the way, it's best not to point this out to the person who is complaining but simply to remain sympathetic, to remain a friend.)

The reason forgiveness as usually practiced doesn't work is that the underlying dynamic has not been eradicated, and each new grievance feeds the fundamental belief that the situation is hopeless.

The common approach to forgiveness is to look at what one's partner is doing, or not doing, and attempt to rationalize why this action is understandable or why it should not be taken so seriously. It is something we say to ourselves but don't really believe. The mind divides itself into pro and anti forgiveness and merely argues with itself. Using the mind in this way will at best yield only temporary relief. This is because one's focus is still on one's partner and not on oneself.

The approach to forgiveness that I would like to suggest is to take your partner out of the equation altogether. Forget your partner. Do not hover over them mentally, analyze their motives, keep track of their transgressions, or even wonder what they are up to now.

This does not mean that you withdraw emotionally; in fact, it is essential to be kind, to be present, to be a friend. The "new" approach makes kindness *more* likely, because you are not conflicted. If your aim is unified, conflict is impossible.

The only question becomes, what is *your* ego up to now? So instead of focusing on your partner, focus on your mental health and inner tranquility. Make your own peace your sole preoccupation.

This is actually as simple as it sounds. Anytime a negative thought about your partner comes to mind, consider your own mindset and what you can do to make it whole. What state do you want your mind to be in? This is quite different than arguing against the thought.

The technique is this: pause and feel your inner stillness and wholeness — to whatever degree you can at the moment — then bring the negative thought into this calmness. Notice that when you do this, the grievance, the painful memory, or the negative emotion soon begins to dissolve.

It doesn't matter whether your partner "deserves" this. It doesn't matter whether your friends would call their actions unforgivable. Only the health of *your* mind, and not meting out justice, is your new concern.

The negative thought about your partner may return many times, but just persist in this new way. Decide to out-endure your ego. Bringing negative thoughts into the light of your own heart can feel strange or even abnormal, because many of us are used to pushing them away. The old approach was to deny negativity, to reject it. The new way is to see your shadow side clearly but not to fear it. You deliberately and in detail "cast light" on it. Then be confident that shadows disappear in light.

Once again, your goal is not to change your mind about your partner or whomever else you are working to forgive. Your goal is to protect your own inner wholeness and peace. This anyone can learn to do — if they will practice. And the resulting miracle is that whatever underlying dynamics exist begin to dissolve into peace and oneness, at least within you and surprisingly often within your partner as well. So set your partner free. Now your purpose is to be your Self.

THE FUNCTION OF
GRANDPARENTS AND PARENTS

When Gayle and I phoned my mother to tell her that Gayle was pregnant with our first child, she got in her car and drove across town to tell us not to expect her to babysit, because she would not be doing "any of that." She may have said some nice things, too, and probably did, but we registered nothing after her jolting pronouncement.

My mother never babysat and we never asked her to, although when John reached five, she did enjoy taking him to her studio and teaching him how to sculpt.

We can all look back on our lives and see many missed opportunities to make ourselves happy. I believe that in her final days my mother had shed enough of her selfishness that if she had it to do over, she would have opened her arms to all her grandchildren, which would have made her very happy.

The function of grandparents is to love without hesitation or reservation. Grandparenting is the process of learning *how* to love another as yourself. This means that you must let go of all desire to pressure, advise, take sides, or influence the parents, because pure love never tries to control. Even if the child is being spanked, as excruciatingly distressful as it would be (and we know a minister who recently found himself in this circumstance), unless the grandchild is in physical danger, grandparents only make matters worse by inserting themselves, and they risk being cut off from spending time with the child, which the child now needs more than ever.

Certainly, no grandparent should spank a child or use other harsh punishments themselves, and if the parents make this an issue, a loving grandparent must remain steadfastly harmless. Perhaps they can fudge a little and say, "You know, that child is perfectly behaved around us. You're so lucky to have a kid who never seems to need disciplining." If this or other ploys don't work, the grandparents must still do no harm, even if this means losing their grandparenting privileges.

I was punched by my dad, but somehow the spankings I received from my father's parents felt like a deeper and more shocking betrayal and ultimately destroyed my love for them.

Anger toward a child is always a mistake. Kindness is intuitive and healing and truly helpful. The function of grandparents, as well as parents, is to reflect the unshakable devotion they have felt from God and that they know will be there always.

PRACTICING INNOCENCE BRINGS FREEDOM

Forgiving ourselves is a hard one. It may even be more difficult than forgiving others. One reason is that we think of it as a form of humility. We may even be a little proud that we are "hard" on ourselves. In sports, for example, you often hear the statement that a coach is hard on players, "but they are even harder on themselves."

There is also the deeper, less conscious thought that if we forgive ourselves, we will be forced to forgive everyone else. And this we are reluctant to do.

Regardless of what makes it difficult, it is essential to forgive ourselves if we are ever to see who we are at our core. It is impossible to extend love while feeling shame or embarrassment. Guilt demands that we first withdraw into smallness.

Acknowledging our past hurtful acts and seeing the damage they have done can be motivation for changing the direction of our lives. And the power of this form of self-examination cannot be overstated. But once it is done, the choice now is what we are going to do about it. To remain mired in guilt is merely a way of procrastinating having to face that choice.

A mistake does not need to be made into a sin; it needs to be seen and corrected. This is what personal integrity asks of me.

It is what my loved ones ask of me. It is what life asks of me. To love ourselves may seem selfish, or at least the ego tells us that it is selfish, but it opens the door to forgiving others.

Believe that you are guilty and you will believe others are as well. Guilt, like love, is a complete mindset. Even in a play-group, if one parent suddenly sees another child as guilty, within moments that parent is often irritated at their own child. You simply can't love one person while seeing another as guilty at the same time, yet very few people believe this concept. They believe deeply in the possibility of selective guilt. Since seeing guilt or seeing innocence can only be done in the moment, why not just alternate? Love a little, hate a little, depending on circumstances. That approach does seem to fit the nature of how the day unfolds better than just deciding on forgiveness and sticking with it.

The reason this is an unsatisfactory approach is that griev-ances usually don't go away without a lot of work, and al-though on occasion they may be dismissed quickly in a playgroup, most of us not only harbor them — we actually cherish them, sometimes for years. Sadly, this infects our perception of the world.

Since feeling guilt leads to seeing it, just as seeing it leads to feeling it, whether we begin with our own God-created innocence or with the innocence that eternally abides in others, practicing innocence brings freedom. Heaven on Earth is merely a place where innocence is seen inside and out.

THERE ARE NO QUESTIONS
IN GOD

The Heart Shrine Relic Tour recently came to Tucson. Among other sacred objects, it included over a thousand pearl-like beads, said to be from the cremated remains of the Buddha and several of his disciples.

These were exhibited in a series of shrine-like displays on a single table. In a silent, candlelit room, our family moved slowly around the display along with other non-Buddhists and Buddhists. On the day we came, over two thousand people attended.

Before leaving, each person who wished to participate was individually blessed by a monk, who gently touched the head of the one kneeling before him with a stupa (in this case a small, sacred relic). A small container of saffron water, taken from the bowls containing the relics, was handed out as we left. The water symbolizes the seeds of loving-kindness and can be used to bless anyone or anything.

We felt changed by the experience — and everyone we talked to reported the same — although I am sure there must have been people who did not.

No one in our family knew whether the "pearls" were what they were believed to be, the monks who blessed us were obviously very tired, we had trouble ferreting out our shoes in the pile at the door, and none of us had any particular knowledge or understanding of Buddhism.

Yet we were changed. We felt a deep peace and oneness that we had seldom felt before.

The point I want to make is that I have no point to make. I don't know why this happened and have never felt any real curiosity about it.

Perhaps it is as simple as this: there are no questions in God.

REST

If the Truth is true, there is nowhere to go and nothing to do. To choose stillness is to rest in God.

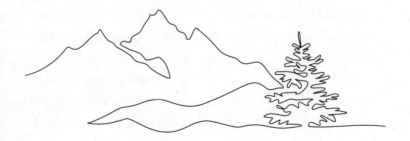

Infatuation Is Not Love

At this time in our culture, infatuation is treated as almost a sacred part of one's self and going against it a form of self-betrayal. You often hear people say, "You can't help what you feel." Nothing could be further from the truth.

Infatuation is not unlike any of the other ego emotions. It, too, is generated by focus. Change the focus and you change the emotion.

Infatuation is often mistaken for love, because it is often the primary emotion felt when one first meets one's future husband or wife; usually infatuation is replaced by the reality of married life, parenting, and so forth. Counselors frequently hear that "the magic has gone out of my marriage." What has actually left the marriage is not "magic" but infatuation, which can never be sustained. You can be infatuated with a new car, but it doesn't last; what about that new house that you were ecstatically raving about only a few years ago? Believing in the sustainability of infatuation is an enormous mistake that may lead an individual to consider betraying their partner if they meet someone new who seems to have everything that is missing in their husband or wife. Infatuation, being solely their own desire, is not compelling them to do or think about anything. If you wish to be rid of the feeling of infatuation, the procedure is quite simple — if you are sure you want to change it, because infatuation can be profoundly addictive.

I stress being sure, because if you are conflicted about being free of infatuation, then nothing you do will help. So first you need to get clear that you *want* to be free. It is also crucial to remember that you want to take as much time as is necessary to become clear, because betraying your marriage will upend not only your life but the lives of many others. Take all the time you need, and don't give up.

It can be helpful to spend a day or two, or even a few weeks, being honest with yourself and looking deeply into your heart. What do you really want? What kind of person do you want to be? What do you think will make you feel better about yourself? How do you want to treat others? How important is God to you?

It is important to recognize that ridding your mind of an infatuation can be extremely difficult, because we tend to accept our feelings as the truth; if we feel it, it must be real. You may feel hopeless even thinking about removing this infatuation from your life or believe that even if you do, you will then be faced with a marriage that has lost its "magic" forever. However, that is merely what the ego would have you believe. Our egos love chaos and misery!

So, what do you do? First, remind yourself that feelings change and can't always be trusted. If possible, remember a time when you had a strong feeling about someone else or something else, only to realize that your infatuation was ridiculous; all of us have extensive experience with that. Begin each day determined not to betray yourself or your partner. When your ego presents you with thoughts about how your infatuation is justified and real, sit down, turn to your peaceful mind, and just let those thoughts float away. Don't argue with them; release them. See this as freeing your mind to see clearly ... without infatuation, judgment, or anger.

Obviously, it's best to arrange your life so that you have absolutely no contact with the individual with whom you are infatuated, but if there are times when this is not feasible, whenever you are near this person, and even if you aren't sure you believe it at this moment, remind yourself that these feelings of infatuation are temporary.

Infatuation is the mind focusing exclusively on only one set of idealized data. It is a form of self-hypnosis. So, this emotion can definitely be manipulated. Here are two suggestions for living with infatuation while not acting on it:

1. When you experience the emotion, take a moment to just stare at it, noting what it feels like, where it manifests in your body, what color it reminds you of, what texture, and so on. Examine it in minute detail. This type of meditation will change the emotion within moments. Repeat this procedure as often as necessary.

2. When you are in a situation, because of time or circumstances, where you can't do any of the above, just be *peacefully* infatuated. Even though it doesn't "feel" like it, infatuation is fear based and is accompanied by a variety of worries about the past and future. Your peaceful mind is always with you and can be turned to during any emotional episode. The Source of true pleasure is with you now and can be invited into your heart at any time.

You *are* your peaceful mind. Peace is your strength and your destiny. Peace has already offered, and you have already received, everything.

Happy Conversations

Friends are not for venting. To occasionally vent is OK. It's nice to have someone you can talk to and trust with difficult problems and in return provide an understanding ear when that is what your friend needs. But to view a friend as simply someone who is willing to hear your endless complaints misuses love. Yet many friendships develop this one-sided dynamic. I complain; you listen. A real conversation is a sharing of mutual caring. We see, we listen, and we hear. These are the gifts we give to each other. Healthy and happy conversations are not consistently dominated by one person.

On Gossip

Ordinary conversations are mostly gossip. And quite innocent. Gossip is interesting and fun and often makes you laugh. We look forward to seeing a friend just to get "the latest gossip." So why does it have such a bad reputation?

Because, like most human activities, there is more than one kind. History is mostly gossip. The news is mostly gossip. Gossip is a great fundraiser for political campaigns. Gossip can unjustly destroy a public figure. And more to the point, we can use gossip to betray confidences and to poison one person against another. These forms of gossip are highly destructive and block all hope of real relationship.

But as to everyday gossip, please, please, please don't stop gossiping in the name of trying to be more spiritual.

How to Argue in Peace: The Ten Steps

It is not a mistake to argue, but it's a tragic mistake to have repeated arguments that do nothing but weaken your relationship.

This was happening to Gayle and me early in our marriage, so we worked out a procedure that reversed this dynamic. We named it "How to Argue in Peace." It worked so well that later we began teaching it in workshops. Below are the basic steps.

I might first add that if you have a partner who is unwilling to try the steps, you can do them yourself by setting up two chairs and picturing your partner in the other chair. Just be certain to get up and become your partner before answering yourself back.

1. The first step is to decide on an issue. In order to begin learning this process as an ongoing tool for bridging rifts, you might want to tackle only what seems to be a minor issue the first time or two you do this. Later it will become clear that anything that divides you is never minor, but at first perhaps stay away from things that are highly charged emotionally. What you want is the *experience* of success.

It is surprising how many couples have never had a successful argument.

2. We love to combine so many things into one problem that it can't be solved, so take the issue and divide it into its component parts. For example, say the issue is that one of you tends to run later than the other when you are going out. Actually, that has several parts. One may be a sense of when it is best to arrive. Another may be that one person feels compelled to check that doors are locked and lights are out, and the other person seldom helps with this. Another may be that there is a running disagreement on how long it takes to travel certain distances. Another, how much leeway should be given for unforeseen traffic conditions. Still another, what social obligations should be honored. And so forth.

   So, take just one of the components and work on that alone.

3. Set up two chairs facing each other. Sit for a moment with your eyes closed and see clearly that you do not want this or anything else to divide you.

4. In turn, you each state your *ego* position on the issue. Give only your side of it. Do not throw in spiritual-sounding ideas of how you understand your partner's position, or gratuitous compliments, or acknowledgments of your own mistakes.

Also, do not bring up any other issue, past mistakes, or any criticisms. It is important to stick to this one issue only. Therefore, state your ego position without embellishment.

5. Do not interrupt.

6. While your partner is talking, silently repeat to yourself, *[Name] really means this*. Our ego does not believe that our partner means what to us is so obviously wrong or unfair or distorted. We think they have an ulterior motive. But they do mean it, and if we will listen carefully, we will understand what they mean.

7. Restate your ego positions. But this time *only* in terms of what you personally are afraid of. Fear is on a deeper level, so it is good to take a moment to quietly think of what your fears are around this specific issue.

When you are ready, state these fears to each other. Listen carefully and believe each other. Step 7 is so powerful that it alone can sometimes resolve the issue. Here are two examples.

The issue between one couple was that she was a gourmet cook who loved to give elaborate parties, yet he would attend dressed in blue jeans and a T-shirt. In getting in touch with their fears, he saw that he was afraid that if he gave in to her pressure to dress more formally, this would eventually lead to his losing his independence and individuality. She, on the other hand, was afraid that the way he dressed showed a lack of respect for her. If he really loved her, he would dress the way she asked.

In discussing their fears, he realized that for her these parties were an important creative outlet that she was very good at. She, on the other hand, saw that his fear of losing his identity was deeply felt and was not a lack of respect for her. The result was that in step 9, when they exchanged their gifts, hers was to let him wear whatever he wanted and his was to wear what was appropriate. They had both realized that they wanted to help each other with their fears.

Another couple had a running argument over when the husband took out the composting material. She felt that he often waited too long despite repeated promises to be timelier. When looking at their fears, they uncovered a similar dynamic to that of the previous couple. He felt that her making such a big issue of what to him was a small matter was just the beginning of her agenda to remake him and that if he adhered strictly to the schedule she had laid out, he would eventually lose all sense of who he really was. She felt that if she couldn't trust him with such a simple task, what could she trust him with? He didn't even respect her enough take out compost as promised.

Once each realized how deep the fears were behind a seemingly silly issue, they both *wanted* to drop their ego stands. Which they in fact did. He now tries hard to be punctual, and if he slips up, she never mentions it. *The key was seeing that they did not want their partner to be afraid.*

8. Close your eyes and think of ten things about your partner that you like. As much as possible, link these to specific incidents in which your partner was kind, funny, patient, or thoughtful, or just things you like about them: how they laugh, some physical feature you're partial to, or any cute or endearing things they have done.

   Open your eyes and take turns trading these compliments back and forth. Pay no attention to who takes the longest to think of things. It does not mean that the slower person is thinking more deeply about their answers or that the faster person loves more. It doesn't mean anything except that we each have a different process.

9. Close your eyes and think of three gifts that you want to give to this relationship. Perhaps think of these as three building blocks. You are building a stronger, more beautiful relationship.

   It is essential that each of the gifts relates specifically to the one issue under consideration. This is not a competition. Do not make broad professions of love or unrealistic offers of generosity. Be specific. This is very important. What three things would your partner think of as a real gift regarding *this* issue?

Open your eyes and share your gifts.

10. Last, do not monitor your partner to see if they are following through. Just do your part.

Granted, in our workshops we were there to help lead the couples through this process, but in the thirty years we have been doing this we have yet to see a couple fail to make substantial progress, and most couples who have done it on their own report resolving their issue on the spot.

The reason for the success is quite simple. The issue is held within the ego mind, but the ego, believing absolutely in separation, does not have the tools to argue in a way that increases oneness. But when the couple switches to their joined mind, they have all the insight they could possibly need.

Sometimes during step 7, but always during step 8, the switch takes place. Everyone in the group notices this. The couple starts smiling and sometimes giggling. They are beginning to feel their oneness, and this makes them happy. Following this up with gifts to the one they now see that they understand rather than oppose comes easily. They have made their relationship more important than the issue.

So, What Do You Do?

The thought that, like a soulmate, the "right" job is waiting for us can make the search for work painfully stressful and plant the fear that the job we end up taking is probably not "the one." The truth is that few of us end up doing what our studies in high school and/or college prepared us for. Gayle and I are typical; we both got teaching certificates but only taught one year each. It takes a unique talent plus almost supernatural patience to be a good teacher, and neither of us had those.

Parents who plant the fear that future happiness depends on choosing the right occupation do their children a disservice. The belief that there are inferior jobs drives people to question their self-worth and keeps them from committing completely to what they are doing now. No one should base their identity on a job description. Yet in our society the question "So, what do you do?" often means "Are you somebody?" A professional athlete is given far more attention, money, and praise than a schoolteacher; yet a schoolteacher is in a position of equal if not greater potential impact on other people's lives.

Even the image of "having a career" does not fit most people's lives. Among other things, I have been a real-estate broker, a Christian Science practitioner, a lecturer, a construction worker, a minister, a guidance counselor, and a ranch hand. Any of these would qualify as a career if carried on "long enough." I am also a parent and a husband. Some might argue that those two jobs are not careers.

Trying, along with Gayle, to raise two boys to become decent human beings who will be happy, unafraid, and kind is more the work of a lifetime than having been the cofounder of a church. When you consider all the lives theirs will touch, two good human beings affect the world more extensively and positively than "preaching to the choir."

I mention all of this because I encounter so many people on a spiritual path who think that they have not yet found their calling. Their calling is to *be* spiritual, not to have a job description that *sounds* spiritual. Their calling is to work at their job with grace and integrity, not to vanquish coworkers. Their calling is to take each task as it comes and not look longingly past it to the next task. It is to do what is before them now with commitment and peace, and to do it well.

Some people look forward to their workday and some to their workday ending. Yet barring those few who have inherited or already made a great deal of money, everyone has to earn a living. Many feel locked into the job they have because of the potential financial deterioration or even disaster they risk should they try to change jobs. They may have family members depending on them, or they may feel that they are already barely meeting their own basic needs. So off to work they go. At least they have a job, so they try to make the best of a less-than-ideal situation.

A great many people genuinely enjoy their occupation but, interestingly, they are a statistical minority. Let's first consider individuals who are deeply aware of feelings and thoughts. Although often making good managers because of their perception of individual dynamics, they also, as would be expected, pick up the collective discord and anxious lines of thought that surround them. Since these are part of the general atmosphere, they often don't know from whom the thoughts are coming or toward whom they are directed. Therefore, their tendency is to internalize these feelings and become somewhat paranoid, distressed, or judgmental. This mindset is then carried home at night and pollutes the home atmosphere.

Even people who are not especially aware can nevertheless be strongly affected by grudges and infighting between co-workers. It is difficult for them to remain untouched when merely *witnessing* a feud, even if not personally involved. And to be excluded from the cliques that often form is obviously painful; yet to be included can engender guilt. These experiences of separation are also held in the mind when the individual leaves work.

In both cases finding a way to put in place a mental shield can lessen the effects of the more difficult circumstances you will encounter today. One effective game is to become a cog in the machine — an excellent cog but a cog nonetheless.

It's sort of like putting on a work uniform before you arrive at your job. The uniform represents your specific function. You thus acknowledge that you have a function, a defined role that those you work for expect from you, but sacrificing your mental peace is not part of it. Specifically, you will not take on other individuals' dramas or the emotional entanglements of the business as a whole. You will listen and be understanding, you will do your part and do it well, but you will not mentally change your reason for being at work. You will continue to be a cog.

It's not that you refuse to hear complaints, gossip, and criticisms, but you don't take them to heart. You consign them to the general hum of the machine, the machine of business.

Most importantly, as you leave work, you consciously and deliberately remove your "uniform," your "cogness," so that by the time you reach home, you are again fully and freely yourself.

Once you have learned how to encase yourself in your purpose for being at work, you are now ready to commit completely to the job. There are several definitions of *commitment*, but the one you want is very similar to commitment to a partner. A job is in fact a partnership, and you want the same attitude you would have toward a wife or husband. You will know you are committed to your job when you appreciate it, appreciate having it and being in it, and especially when you feel a genuine desire to be helpful to the people you are associating with, just as you want to be of true help to your own partner.

There are, of course, other strategies that can help make a less-than-pleasant job more bearable, even enjoyable. Many articles and books are devoted to this subject, but one point that should go without saying is that if you are being abused, half measures will not work, and you should extricate yourself from the abuse in any way necessary.

Here are also some of the more familiar and time-tested work-related suggestions you may have heard before:

1. Stay in the present.

2. Consciously practice acceptance. (You get in the current of the river and flow with it.)

3. Forgive quickly by monitoring your thoughts and surrounding in light anyone who occupies a disturbed place in your mind.

4. Notice that individuals who are particularly vexing are always undergoing subtle changes. Predicting how someone will be the next time you encounter them and then comparing that to how they actually are can help relax and broaden your attitudes.

5. Look for good intentions.

6. Practice simple kindness.

To Touch the Sky

They say that out there one can touch the sky. Yet here my shell is as familiar as an eyelid. It is small but entirely mine. I sense the warmth of love above and around me, but where does that come from? I can't see it through the shell. I would need blind faith to peck through. I would need an unknown future. I would need a still and empty mind. I would need a self I have never known. Only then could I touch the sky.

GOOD LUCK

Good luck only scares you. The longer it lasts, the more you wait for the other shoe to drop.

Although the media sprinkles in a few cheery stories about unlikely heroes and rescued puppies, for the most part it offers a steady diet of fear and disaster. Swallow news stories for an hour or two each day and you can't help concluding that misfortune rains down on most people, be they special or ordinary.

But suddenly, for you, everything is going your way. You are elated, yet there is this one small nagging thought. The Karma police are watching. They are keeping track of all these favorable happenings, and soon the imbalance will be corrected. Circumstances that should be making you happy are increasingly a cause for concern.

And is it even *moral* for you to have good fortune when everyone around you seems to be having problems? True, most people you encounter point out that these annoyances or outrages are not their fault, but at the moment you can't think of anything comparable in your own life. Where is the equality in that? Where is the justice?

Furthermore, where is the safety?

If you aren't worried, your guard is down. You should be recalling things that have gone wrong and cataloging likely snares on the path to come. Wipe that smile off your face and study the shadows. Who knows what is in all those dark corners?

Yet the bad things in our past keep shifting and changing. As time passes, we reappraise what happened. Was a past event an affliction, or did it build character? Did some grievous mistake diminish us, or did it lead to a welcome career change or possibly a bright new friendship? If the latter, which events would we now change, and what would *their* unintended consequences be?

Characterizing the past is a tricky business. An honest person admits that it isn't always clear what is harmful. This would also have to apply to the present. It follows that we probably don't know what should or should not happen next.

Which brings us back to good luck. You would think it would be enough that we like the way things are going. Surely we are not sophisticated, intelligent, or realistic merely because we can find ways to sabotage our happiness.

It's a mistake to believe that happiness is a perilous state of mind, even happiness caused by good luck. A naturally happy mind — as opposed to a mind on which optimism has been dishonestly forced — is in a better position to recognize love and to choose behavior that leads to peace. The more anxious a mind, the narrower and tighter it tends to be. A happy mind is relaxed. It looks around more easily. It is open to more options. And it may unexpectedly generate one or two more measures of good luck.

Honesty

Early in our marriage, Gayle and I realized that we sometimes hurt each other's feelings when we got an honest
answer to the question "Do you like it?" after fixing one of
our favorite dishes. So, we made a rule: "If you can keep it
down, the answer is yes." And no matter how closely ques-
tioned, you did not back down. That little gambit turned an
unhappy dynamic into a running joke.

This is the same category of questions as "Does this make
me look fat?" Or "Do you think I talk too much?" Or "Does
the ferret like you better than me?"

Today you are thought to be lying if your words are not lit-
erally accurate. But it wasn't always that way. The concept of
the "white lie" took into account the person's real motive for
asking the question and, especially, how the person would
interpret the words you said in response. In other words, it
added love.

If someone said to us, "Don't you think that what so-and-so
did to me was outrageous?" we understood that the real
question was "Do you support me? Are you my friend?"
And so, we didn't launch into a lecture on seeing the other
person's side of things. Because that wasn't the real question.

It's not whether or not to lie but whether or not to listen.
If we truly listen, and if our heart is in the right place, our

words will convey a deeper honesty that answers a deeper question.

And then there is lying to ourselves. Perhaps this is the greatest spiritual mistake we can make. It is the one area that demands deep, absolute, constant honesty. You have no hope of going in a consistent direction if you don't weed out every habit of kidding yourself. At first this practice can be difficult and unpleasant, but it eventually leads where all inward honesty leads: the gentle and lovely truth of who you are.

An ancient Navajo prayer puts it this way:

> *With beauty before me may I walk.*
> *With beauty behind me may I walk.*
> *With beauty below me may I walk.*
> *With beauty above me may I walk.*
> *With beauty all around me may I walk.*

Lighten Up

For the first year or so of life, we communicate without words. "Crying is the first sonic message of the infant," states one authority (although I can think of one or two other unequivocal baby sounds).

Empathetic parents learn to distinguish between a "sleepy cry," a "hungry cry," an "angry cry," and so forth. Later, parents teach toddlers nouns through repetition. Each new name the child mimics is an occasion for celebration that delights both parent and child.

So far so good.

Most of us come into the world valuing oneness over separation, and that makes us happy. Children see fewer strangers than adults. And in most little kids, happiness is irrepressible. It can bubble up at any moment for no good reason. I believe that is one explanation for why so many adults smile at small children. Those who are happy, without even knowing it, extend an invitation to people and pets to join in. But also, just seeing innocence (and all children are innocent) makes us feel good, a lesson we resist transferring to other areas of our life.

As they do with most activities — getting ready for bed, eating with utensils, and so on — toddlers use speaking as an opportunity to have fun. Yet during the toddler stage we also begin to see the first signs of conflicting perspectives between adult and child over the function of language. For example, most little kids quickly discover that the word *no* isn't any fun at all.

This being a world in which all things tend toward separation, adults eventually win this battle with their kids over the true function of language. As children grow up, their instinct to use words inclusively gives way to fear of the consequences for not using words to defend their self-interest.

"Let's have fun" eventually becomes "What's in it for me?" even though our mind dresses it up in loftier thoughts about honoring our individuality, our pride, and our rights.

"The point I want to make" is a concept foreign to most kids, yet it's the hallmark of arguments between partners. If the intention is to understand and identify with our partner, the words that come out of our mouth can be trusted. However, if the intention is to prove a point and be right, almost anything we say — no matter how many keys to communication we have memorized — consistently yields disappointing results.

Just as little children's attempts to get adults to lighten up are sometimes met with stiff resistance, so, too, our attempts to be kind can go unappreciated. But does that mean we stop making them? Now we come face-to-face with the question of what true maturity is. Certainly, it is not to run around, play, and scream, as is the function of little kids. But it does no harm to ask why they do that. Isn't it because they are happy and filled with energy and like to stir the happiness pot? *Why all this boring shopping for the same things? Why not run up and down aisles and find fun things to eat and play with?* No, true maturity for an adult would not be doing that. And it would make a lot of people angry.

True maturity is becoming like a little child, but in attitude, not in behavior. Children teach us how to overlook off-putting physical characteristics, how to stay in the present, how to forgive quickly, how to search almost any activity for something enjoyable, and how to laugh easily.

The way it is usually practiced, maturity is a form of self-absorption. It is keen social self-consciousness. It is proper and right and appropriate. It is what fits in nicely, and it usually makes us feel important. But the maturity taught by kids is almost the opposite. It is abandonment to a world where a dancing light can be seen, if we would only look for it in humility.

In Prayer, in Meditation

In prayer, one turns for help and thereby acknowledges that help is already there.

In meditation, one turns to the help that is already there and thereby acknowledges that turning is necessary.

To rank one over the other is without charity, and charity is the help.

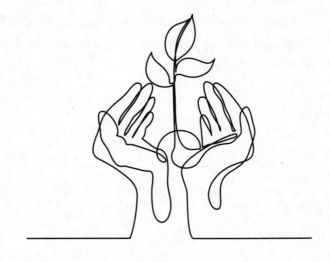

THE FIFTY-FIFTY MYTH

Given the attitude of our times toward "true love," it's surprising that only 25 to 30 percent of those *already* married will get divorced.

And yet, despite this relatively promising prospect, there is now such deep disbelief in love (as opposed to hormonally based attraction) that it has become a social pathology.

Physical attraction can temporarily overcome cynicism about love and provide a couple a short breathing space, but the realities of what it takes to build a real relationship become obvious sooner or later.

Perhaps the statistical effect of the current anti-commitment mindset can best be seen on couples who got married only in the last year or two. These individuals' chances of staying married are around 60 percent. As even a brief Google search will show, the myth that half of all marriages end in divorce is based on a flawed statistical analysis that occurred in the 1980s.

There are so many factors to consider when analyzing divorce data that no two experts agree on a couple's exact chance of staying together, but very few authorities say it even approaches fifty-fifty. No matter how you look at it, the odds of a marriage lasting are greater than the odds of it ending in divorce.

The unfortunate effect of the fifty-fifty myth is that couples start out with a sense of doom. Add to this the media's obsession with celebrity divorce and psychology's decades-long emphasis on ego protection and reinforcement, and you end up with a widespread fear of commitment that tends to manifest as soon as there are difficulties in the marriage. And there *will* be difficulties.

Even a hint within a profile on a dating site that a person wants a permanent relationship is off-putting and will significantly reduce interest. The fear of entanglement is now greater than the desire for commitment.

The current situation is so toxic that couples frequently do better when they drop marriage as a goal and focus instead on developing a real relationship. Interestingly, this approach often leads to a wedding ceremony more quickly, because the marriage service is now seen as a byproduct of a deeper, more enduring goal. In my opinion, individuals should commit to accepting a potential partner (or an existing spouse) as they are. Acceptance is the road to a real relationship, not marriage.

However, as an ancient symbol, the marriage ceremony itself can be quite helpful — if it follows the necessary groundwork — because it outwardly ratifies what is inwardly sacred. But the groundwork comes first.

Many individuals make the mistake of trying to pressure their partner into getting married. This approach tends to increase the other person's resistance, since most people don't like being told what to do. And if a marriage does occur, the pressure that brought it about usually sets up several unnecessary problems.

Individuals who win such a battle soon discover that their expectations of what it would be like to be married are not met, and those who were pressured feel resentful and seek out evidence that they were right to have resisted. Perhaps an even greater problem — especially given the current disbelief in love — is that when the couple goes through difficult times, they are more likely to start wondering whether the marriage was a mistake from the beginning.

The person who did the pressuring thinks, *My partner never loved me to begin with or else they would have wanted marriage.* And the one who resisted thinks, *I knew this was a bad idea from the start.*

The most successful approach to the question of whether to get married is for both individuals to wait until there is a mutual sense of peace about the decision. Naturally, if one partner doesn't care much one way or the other, and being married is extremely important to the other partner, they should probably get married.

About ten years ago a friend of ours who had gone through two divorces suddenly found herself in a relationship with a man with whom she was very comfortable. They both loved the same sports and activities and spent so much time together that they eventually started living together.

However, our friend was confronted with two problems. Her partner was a conservative and she was a progressive, and it seemed important to her to defend her political positions. And secondly, he had also been divorced and had made it clear from the beginning that he never wanted to get married again, whereas she did.

Realizing that their relationship was good on many levels, our friend decided to stop arguing — or teasing — about politics. She also made up her mind never again to bring up marriage.

As so often happens when we truly let go, the events of her life began to reflect her more peaceful state of mind. They grew more understanding of each other's politics and showed their respect by not raising divisive issues. Then one evening he fixed dinner for the two of them and hid an engagement ring at the bottom of her wineglass.

Luckily, although she didn't see it, she didn't swallow it, and the marriage that followed has only enhanced their bond.

Acceptance doesn't ensure specific results, but it does ensure a more peaceful outcome.

Mindfulness

Mindfulness is simply sensing that where you stand is holy ground. It is the knowledge that each little thing you do is an opportunity to bring stillness to your mind.

The mistake is thinking that being mindful is a special activity set apart from ordinary life. Correctly seen, it is a practice period for how we want to live.

The mind wanders off; we gently bring it back to what matters. The mind wanders off; we gently bring it back to what matters. And what does matter?

To what do we bring it back? To the present. To being at peace now. To feeling connected now. To loving now.

CHEATING

Notice that every object in your dwelling — each picture, chair, rug, appliance, doodad — has a little story. As you walk past your stuff, your stuff talks to you. It is subtle, but notice that each thing your eyes land on evokes a memory. You don't just live with furnishings; you live with your past actions regarding each of them. This also applies to the bodies who live with you, be they person or pet. If you cheated, betrayed, stole, or tricked to get anything around you, you may not believe you are in hell, but you can certainly hear it.

WHAT ARE YOU WORTH?

When seeking help, couples often give graphic details about their sex problems, but if money is the issue, when asked how much they make, the couple balks. It has always been fascinating to Gayle and me that what you are "worth" is considered more personal than what you want your partner to do in bed.

In the West, money is closely linked to identity. We are what we earn. Those who see themselves as "better-off" often feel superior. Those who think of themselves as poor tend to look down on themselves and, if they have families, may even believe they are failures.

Rarely will people who have great wealth fail to display it. The wealthy often buy things they don't need and can't use. They may have houses they rarely visit, cars they seldom drive, and closets full of clothes they rarely wear. The underlying thought is *What's the use in having money if there are no signs that you have it?*

So universal is this attitude that when it's discovered after their death that someone who lived modestly all their lives was worth millions, the story makes national news.

Although only one of many possible issues within relationships, differences over money set up one of the most common and destructive dynamics. There are many couples who escape this, but not the majority. The potential harm to friendships, families, businesses, and places of worship is similar.

Setting aside severe addiction, chronic abuse, and lack of commitment — since it could be argued there was no real relationship to begin with — in most cases money issues are more affecting than poor communication, a death in the family, and even infidelity.

As has been said for thousands of years, it is not money itself that is the problem. After all, money is just pieces of paper, metal disks, or numbers on a computer screen. That said, there are few subjects that can reverse one's spiritual direction more quickly than a sudden concern over money, because love is exchanged for fear.

It is fine to say to someone "just turn it over to God," but for most people demonstrating this kind of faith in the face of severe financial difficulty can seem next to impossible. So, what can be done?

Staying in the present helps.

So, for example, I can ask myself, *Regardless of what tomorrow brings, do I have enough this moment?* If I do, nothing prevents me from continuing to ask this question each time this fear comes to mind.

And do I know, with absolute certainty, that the disaster I imagine will happen? Have I been wrong about the future before? If I have, I do not want to continue telling myself that this time I have perfect certainty.

And finally, *Am I sure that, having asked for help from something greater than myself, I will not receive help?* If I believe help is possible, I will not tell what is greater than me in what form that help must come.

I can speak from experience, as can many of you who read this, that when you use a gentle, in-the-present approach such as this, you begin to feel, actually *feel*, what it means to "turn it over to God."

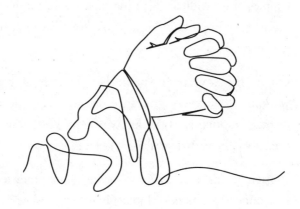

A SMALL PRICE TO PAY

Although what follows is about old friends who are couples, we also all have long-term one-on-one friendships that are special. No matter the category, there's something a little different about the friendships we have had over many years. It has been suggested that some of these did not begin in this lifetime. Maybe that helps describe the added dimension they seem to possess, but clearly many people have a feeling of something having gone before. This is especially true of children concerning their parents and former parents. They voice bits of memory that are hard to dismiss.

I don't want to make too much of this phenomenon, but this depth of connection often makes acceptance and forgiveness a little easier when it comes to old friends, be they couples or individuals. And the capacity for forgiveness this points to is important, because old friends can also be very exhausting.

Oh, the things we put up with. Using couples as an example, we know their every grievance because we've heard these disputes as long as we've known them. We know well the trajectory the verbal sparring will take.

It often begins with kidding. Maybe because they feel safety in numbers, partners will joke about a grievance in a social setting that they would not state directly in private. Since most teasing contains a kernel of annoyance, this soon leads to mocking. Then someone gets loud, or someone emotionally withdraws.

Or maybe a cold front moves in, enveloping all present. As the couple descend the ladder of unhappiness, we can almost predict the exact words each will say to tweak their partner. Inwardly, they throw up their hands, telling themselves they just don't know how to make the other person happy. But isn't it curious that they do know how to make them *un*-happy? Being insight based, knowledge of one without the other is impossible. But since they are dear friends, we don't point this out. We don't, because we are also friends to their *relationship*. We have seen them overcome many things, and we hope that they will eventually come to love each other as unequivocally as we love them.

Old friends or not, why do so many couples repeat the same dynamics month after month, year after year?

Perhaps the pattern is that one partner is addicted to drama and, often unconsciously, says or does something to upset the other partner. In turn, that individual shuts down emotionally or acts out in an unhelpful way.

Another common pattern: One partner thinks that they are basically superior (have more life experience, are more spiritual, have more money, are the best gender) and should be the leader or teacher within the relationship. The other partner revolts against the position they have been put in and attacks back in some passive or aggressive way, such as nagging or turning up the volume.

A third pattern: A partner thinks of themselves as a victim and sets up circumstances to fulfill this belief. The partner who is supposedly victimizing feels unfairly accused and reacts in ways that make matters worse. (Naturally, I am not speaking of physical or sexual abuse, which is another subject entirely.)

In the above examples, the triggering behavior is usually confined to just a few words or actions, ones that have been repeated many times before. Yet the other partner's reaction to these triggers is equally predictable. Seeing how all of this plays out with old friends can be instructive to our own relationships. Gayle and I have found that discussing their mistakes need not be a form of judgment but a study guide about what not to do in our own relationship. With old friends you have a lot of valuable history to work with.

Often the person who triggers the dynamic is thought to be more to blame. Yet there would be no dynamic if there was no response. In fact, what is a trigger in one relationship may be viewed in another relationship as merely amusing, unimportant, or even part of the "guilty" partner's charm.

There are, of course, numerous dynamics that a relationship can fall into besides these three, and almost all partnerships develop at least one or two. These are a mistake, and today many people avoid the mistake by declining to commit to anyone.

But there is an alternative to living alone: acceptance. Most of us have another group of old friends, perhaps an even a larger one, who are comfortable with each other and comfortable to be around. They know their partners' patterns well, and they accept them. This didn't come without persistence, but any couple who has reached the state of acceptance will tell you it was a small price to pay.

Everything Has
Side Effects

A few years ago, I went in to get a broken foot wired up. Just before the anesthesiologist put me out, it occurred to me to ask the nurse what I was scheduled for. She said, "A leg extension." The form said I was Maria Sanchez. I said, "Do I look like Maria Sanchez?" The nurse rushed off to get a second opinion.

When I recently had a colonoscopy, they told me afterward that they had to keep rolling me from side to side because I had a "floppy colon." They said they didn't want to see me again for ten years! This hurt my self-esteem.

I mentioned to Gayle that I had a little bump on my eyelid, and maybe I should have it removed. She said that our dermatologist had removed one from her eyelid (we are one, even in our bumps).

But the dermatologist told me since I had "eyelash involvement," I should see an ophthalmologist, who would have powerful magnifying lenses. The ophthalmologist, to my surprise, booked me into a hospital. The bump was the size of a grain of rice (organic, basmati).

He somberly told me that despite all precautions, I might lose an eyelash.

"A single eyelash?" I asked.

"Yes."

"Will I be able to get an eyelash transplant?"

When he took this question seriously, I knew I was in trouble, and someday I will write a small book about all that went wrong that day in the hospital.

We live in a world where if you leave bread and crackers out overnight, in the morning the crackers are soft and the bread is hard; where your car will never make the noise when you take it in; where if you get some unexpected cash, it's always followed by an unexpected expense; where shoes never fit when you get them home.

It's a mistake to be optimistic. Don't start the day telling yourself that you are going to have a good day. Start by saying, "Today nothing will go right." And then notice how illogical everything is. Laughably so. Notice that your hair can get very moody — even though you've done nothing to offend it. Notice how people take things the wrong way. Notice that as soon as you get one health problem solved, two take its place. Notice that *everything* has side effects.

Give up the useless battle of trying to control the basic nature of the world or trying to control even what is going on right now. And then notice that when you are peaceful, the body's complaints, deadlines, money problems, and relationship difficulties are turned down in volume. They aren't necessarily solved, but they do distract you less.

We can't really do anything about the nature of the world. We also can do very little about our personal story, our human destiny. On that level, what will happen will happen. But we can do something about the tension we experience whenever we think that we should not be where we are or doing what we are doing, that there is something better than now.

But now will be with us always. So, learning how to respond to now is really all there is to learn.

BEING PREOCCUPIED
OR PRESENT

"In airports his preoccupation was people watching, so naturally he missed his flight." (That isn't from a book; I just wanted an excuse to rationalize my behavior.)

Instead of "preoccupation," the mistake could be called "distraction," "being lost in thought," "inattentiveness," or my favorite, "absence of mind."

The inattentive individual is in fact attentive, just not to the present.

Ever try to carry on a conversation with someone who was just going through the motions of listening? My dad was well known in the family for getting on the phone and asking a series of polite questions he had no interest in. We all learned the tactic of answering back with a question. "How's that lovely family of yours?" he would say. "We're fine, Dad, but I want to know, what do you think of that new library statue in the news?"

"It's shaped like a penis." Now here was a subject he could warm to.

The opposite of being preoccupied is being present. But unfortunately, in many of today's self-improvement teachings "staying in the present" has become a fetish. The idea put forth is that all your attention should be focused just on what you are doing, without any thought of what comes next. This, of course, is impossible.

If you are walking, when you lift your foot, you have a plan: to move the foot forward and place it before you. You have even planned to clear the curb, and that is *many* seconds away. If you are eating, when you lift your fork, you have a plan: to skewer a piece of potato. And not just any piece. That crispy little piece with the interesting texture.

All human activity must take the future into account to some degree. And yet we all have a sense of what it means to stay in the present. It is to take what you are doing now and do it peacefully and consciously. It is not necessary to push the concept to its extreme and never budget, never plan a trip, or never schedule the best time for a pregnancy.

To practice being present in a gentle, flexible way has an interesting effect on the mind. It simplifies it. If preoccupation is dwelling within the busy mind, the monkey mind, then "being here now" is dwelling in the quiet, comfortable mind.

As mentioned before, the ego is the sentence layer of the mind. It may seem to be "idle thinking," but there is a pattern, an agenda, to its babblings. Look closely at what appear to be randomly worded thoughts and the overall aim becomes obvious. It is the ego's attempt to make us feel separate, set apart, possibly in an admirable way, possibly as a victim, but always at a distance from others. That is why love immediately wipes out ego activity and relaxes us. When we feel love, worded thoughts give way to experience. Present experience.

To accurately examine how we become preoccupied, we need to move beyond the question of whether we are "paying attention" to what we are doing, to the larger question of the mental quality required to stay focused. Interestingly, reduced mental exertion is more helpful than attempts to increase control. One learns to relax into the present, to settle more comfortably into the moment at hand. Just do what is before you now and do it in peace.

A lovely calmness is available to us when we admit that we are simply doing what we are doing, that we are where we are, that we are *what* we are. Learning to relax dissolves absentmindedness. To be preoccupied requires far more effort than to be present.

Do I Want Resentment, or Do I Want Peace?

Resentment can unquestionably seem justified. Reasonable people might agree that, certainly in *this* instance, it is fully warranted. None of that changes the fact that it is your decision alone to be resentful.

Millions of words have been written about the self-destructive nature of resentment. Simply stated, it is spiritual suicide. And yet we can be free of it at any moment, because regardless of what someone or some circumstance has done to us, how we think about it is still our choice.

Why, then, do I and so many others struggle with what could be so easy? Why have countless steps been outlined for how to be free of resentment? And why are those steps taken daily by thousands of people, and still the problem keeps coming back? In the face of how much excellent material can be found in bookstores, online, and in meetings on this subject, I can only speak for myself.

I know what makes it difficult for me. I am conflicted. I am conflicted about giving up my capacity to resent — even though I can plainly see what it does to me, to those I discreetly attack, and to those who have to live with me.

Over the years my approach to releasing resentment has greatly simplified, because I now realize that my conflict over whether to give it up is the *only* inherent block. So, if conflict is the problem, not being conflicted is the answer.

I no longer try to let go of resentment since that usually leads to more conflict. I work to become clear. If in the present I feel even the slightest bit resentful, whether through memories, fantasies, or direct encounters, I ask myself, *What do you truly want?*

If looked at honestly, resentment is unequivocal as to what *it* wants: to cherish grudges; to be a victim; to be angry, in turmoil; to feel superior; to distrust; to be easily offended; and, strangest of all, to be cut off from the loving connections that could bring us happiness. We underestimate our desire to be miserable.

Do I want that? Is that how I truly want to be? Now remember, I am conflicted, so obviously I do want "that" to some degree.

Or do I want to be free of the resentment du jour this instant? In fact, would I like to be free of all resentment because I have reached a point where I see the hooks (for the world will never stop presenting them) and instantly refuse to rise to the bait?

Do I want resentment, or do I want peace?

What do I want? What do I want now?

JEALOUSY

Jealousy is not suspicion about another. It is doubt in yourself. Every ray of goodness that you add to your light will shine away a little more of this shadow hovering over your soul.

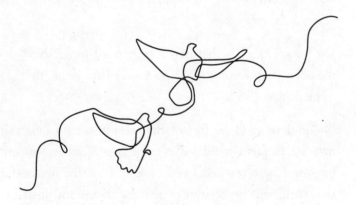

Practicing the Presence

Although making New Year's resolutions often entails under-sized ambitions such as losing ten pounds, it should inspire much weightier goals.

You would think that the practice of listing resolutions for an entire year would suggest that the issues needing attention are those with long-term consequences. And indeed, no matter when we make them, looking at the resolution-making process in that light can be helpful, because a resolution then becomes synonymous with a commitment.

So, the real question is to what should we commit ourselves? For example, we might ask, *What are the blocks holding me back from experiencing lasting peace?*

As luck would have it, that's the very topic I'm about to discuss.

Generally, there are only a few such blocks, and even those are interconnected. They are different versions of one central pattern. The block may be feeling superior or feeling like a victim. It may be fear or guilt. It may be dislike or even hatred manifested in seemingly minor grievances and judgments. To justify hatred, we have to be a victim; when we are a victim, we invariably victimize; when we victimize, we feel superior; when we feel superior, we see guilt; when we see guilt, we are afraid; and so on.

Any ego dynamic viewed in its entirety will not be appealing, and eventually we lose interest in taking this particular bubbling up of our ego seriously. We stop fearing it or acting on it, and even though the same thoughts that used to sabotage our peace are still there, now they are not taken to heart; in fact, we often find them amusing.

Let's face it. If we acted on every ego thought that crossed our minds, we would all be in jail. So, there are many such thoughts that we handle in the correct way. It's the ones we don't that point to the blocks we have erected.

Yesterday was the third night that our overly plump cat Binkley turned up his nose at the expensive low-fat kibble we had just bought. Once again, he complained vociferously all night long. Closing the door was like putting a silk veil over a bullhorn.

Lying sleepless in bed, I thought, *I'm going to kill that cat*. And for a second, I meant it. The next second I saw that he was innocent, and really didn't want to kill him. And I laughed at even having had the thought. This all took less than an instant, because this is the kind of ego chatter I don't take seriously.

Yet when it came to being suddenly and aggressively threatened by the head of the homeowners architectural committee for a violation Gayle and I, who had just moved in, were not even aware of, I nurtured my grievance for several days. Naturally, peace was impossible.

No one talks to me that way is part of my major block, and until I learn to stop being mentally defensive, until I stop fearing that someone's words can diminish me, I will never know a peace that doesn't end.

It is up to the individual to choose peace in place of fear. And here is where resolution comes in. Because the choice *cannot* be forced on you, you must resolve to do it yourself. Yes, you have help, yet no one but you can resolve to accept that help. Until that decision is made, you are locked in a world that becomes increasingly intolerable. None of this is the truth of God, but for you truth is irrelevant because you still have not committed completely to looking at the problem and correcting it. In terms of the world, your anger may be justified, but if you choose justification over peace, you will remain in conflict, and you will not feel the light of God.

It has been my experience that recognizing the problem — seeing and taking responsibility for my primary block — is accomplished in small steps taken in the present. We chip away at the block rather than remove it all at once.

Great spiritual gain can come from, each day, bringing strength, light, and the willingness to decide into that area where we are mentally shut down. Although we often try to make it too complicated to carry out, the approach needed is actually quite simple. It demands merely that we resolve to keep moving in the right direction and to be acutely aware of when we are not.

We take each small challenge as it comes throughout the day, ask for help, and apply what we know as best we can. Our confidence begins to grow, and increasingly we realize that there is One who is always beside us. Our central dynamic does not disappear; we just lose our fear of it. It's no longer a factor. It no longer holds sway. We are free to be who we truly are.

Our ego is like a hand that tightly grips whatever we focus on. Our peaceful mind is like a hand that is relaxed and open. Since the peace of God is a reality, when we choose to be gentle and still, when we choose to be mentally calm and at ease, we start to let go; we start to trust. To that end, here are a few steps I have found helpful.

Taking fear as an example of the kind of block we have been talking about, first it is good to look directly at the specific fear bothering you. It may be helpful to state it out loud or write it down. No harm comes from being specific and observing carefully all the details that come to mind as you simply sit with the fear for a while.

Then remind yourself that now is the only time there is or ever will be. That all of God, all of heaven, is contained within this one eternal instant. That is simply a fact. Perhaps say to yourself, *Nothing prevents me from feeling the presence of my Friend who is with me. Nothing prevents me from feeling comforted this instant. I will be peaceful now.*

As you say these words, allow your mind to move beyond the sentences to the reality they represent. The words themselves hold no magic, but they do point toward something tangible and beautiful.

If these words — or whatever words come to mind — seem phony, recall the resolution you have made. If it seems that you are just mouthing things you don't really believe, simply persist as you have resolved to persist. Maybe you could add, *Be still, little mind. God is with me. My Friend is here to help me with these efforts.*

Note that some measure of tranquility is experienced. Then go about your day as usual until you again feel the fear and the need to pause. Don't worry about how many times you do this. Notice that progress is being made. But more importantly, acknowledge the sacredness of your efforts.

You are practicing the Presence. You are entering heaven. You are in fact doing the only thing that really matters in this lifetime. And therefore, you are fulfilling your destiny, your role, your assignment.

It can take many years to realize that our purpose in this lifetime is entirely mental, and that what we do physically is merely a very small wake we leave behind. Even that wake is temporary, but the gains we make mentally are eternal.

R-E-S-P-E-C-T

Getting respect has become a national obsession. For some, being "disrespected" can be grounds for violence. Ideally, to be respected is to have one's better attributes seen and appreciated, but this is often not the motive behind the need.

When we seek what is usually meant by respect, a little bad temper goes a long way. Many think that people in the service industry respect them more if they are afraid of them. Supervisors often assume that supervisees toe the line better if intimidated. Perhaps more importantly, anger is widely seen as the most direct way of affirming oneself. We fear becoming a doormat if we don't employ it.

Nowadays, it's difficult to make happiness a priority. Happiness is so wussy. Many people, without giving it much thought, assume that what they want most is to control, and happiness is seen as conciliation. They think the most effective way of manipulating people, including their kids and in some cases their partners, is to have a well of irritation and disapproval that can be drawn on at will. The problem is, that well of anger stands in place of our quiet and comfortable center.

Impressive careers in politics, television, radio, and various online formats have been built on intimidation. On the playground, the angry child dominates. If they act out, the unhappy child is more powerful than the happy child. Many spiritual teachers like to think that love is the greatest power on Earth, but even a casual look around shows the opposite to be true in most situations. There are a few Gandhis and Nelson Mandelas, but they are far outnumbered by the bad guys.

Respect based on fear comes with its own set of pleasures. That is why people seek it. It seems to unite the mind, bring us into the present, overcome conflict, give us power, and gain us the deference we deserve.

Only when we look deeper into our episodes of annoyance, umbrage, resentment, and impatience do we see what we sacrifice in not challenging the supremacy of respect and choosing kindness in its place. Examine fear-based respect closely and it is seen as conflict. This is to be expected given that we are betraying what we are at the deepest level.

If in an office, school, governing body, industry, or play-ground some individuals are more respected than others, as is often the case, there is no real oneness, no equality, no "mutual" respect. Certain people always possess more rele-vant talents than others, but it is possible to be very good at what you do without demanding or even wanting acknowl-edgment. Rare but beautiful is the person who feels their connection with, and appreciation for, those around them. Parents, for example, are better at almost everything than their infants, yet it doesn't occur to them to demand respect. As the child grows older, this changes, but it doesn't have to.

What now passes for respect is a mistake. True respect must be earned. It is not the natural outcome of indulging a mood. It comes from kindness and commitment, not from engendering fear. We are most admired and admire ourselves the most when we are consistently fair, decent, and honest. Clearly that does not assure prosperity, good health, political power, or career advancement. But it does allow us to see and express the nature of our soul.

On Hunger

While looking into the refrigerator, if you have to ask your-self if you're hungry, you're not.

Sex Is Not about Sex

Having sex is not a necessity. It may be many things to many people, but it is not an essential part of the natural order. At this time, it is generally necessary for procreation, but it is not an essential tenet of the code of human conduct. And it is definitely not the weather vane of a healthy relationship.

Sex may add to or subtract from oneness, but that will be determined by the reason behind it. For a couple to agree not to have sex at all can just as easily indicate deep love and sensitivity as having sex can symbolize affection and caring.

Couples who successfully incorporate sex into their relationship develop a sex "life." It takes on a rhythm that accommodates and is receptive to the needs of both and is no more an issue than the way they share eating or conversation or entertainment.

To relegate sex to just one of any number of ways of communicating is a horrifying thought for many. This is because the notion that sex is an activity so special that it is, or should be, a mystical experience has become ingrained in us. This in Gayle's and my opinion is utter nonsense, but this general attitude is not without its effects. It is currently generating multiple problems where there need be none at all.

Perhaps the most frequently cited problem with sex is that seldom do two people feel exactly the same about having it at a given moment. This is because sex is not about sex. Like any human activity, it is as nurturing or diminishing as the motive behind it.

Love isn't your partner intuitively knowing what you want. It is more like sharing gifts, and sometimes it is practical and saves time to let your partner know what you would really like to have. It then becomes your partner's pleasure to give this gift to your relationship, and in the giving, much is received.

No one has the license to demand sex of another person, nor is it someone's sacred due to deny sex for trivial reasons or to use it to manipulate. It's not your right to have sex or to withhold it.

However, it is your right to be loving to yourself and to your partner. When deciding whether or not to have sex, partners should ask themselves, *What is best for our relationship at this moment? What approach will promote our oneness?*

THE WORLD DOESN'T
OWE YOU ANYTHING

It's interesting how often fun that is planned isn't fun. Whereas spontaneous fun often turns out to be unexpectedly pleasurable. There are exceptions in both cases, but the assumption that it's always best to schedule fun rather than just let it happen is not consistently borne out by experience.

Consider the thought *Let's take a vacation*. Underpinned by unfounded hope and overlaid with irrational promise, vacations are usually followed by days of physical exhaustion and frayed family relationships and finances. Businesses complain about the effects on their employees of "postvacation syndrome," a term that has even made it into some dictionaries and academic articles.

Many of our happiest moments occur without warning. On the other hand, dinner with friends, weekend Putt-Putt courses, a trip to Dollywood, and building a tree house don't lend themselves easily to spontaneity. Yet they can definitely yield rewards.

Forty-five years ago, Gayle and I got married on the spur of the moment after only two dates, thus avoiding the difficult planning-a-wedding stage. Don't do that. It's way too shocking to your parents.

Twelve years into our marriage, we also made a snap decision to stop using birth control. Our first child was probably conceived within twenty-four hours. Something eerily similar happened with our second child.

Now it's true that in our case the marriage and the children worked out just fine, but this is obviously no way to live your life. Some planning is a good thing. But it does come with its own set of problems.

All would be well if the mind could dispassionately work out a plan (when planning is a rational option) that would simplify life. But humans have this complicating habit of building expectations at the same time that they are laying their plans.

When the idea popped into our minds a few weeks ago to go on an "eating vacation," we already knew that if we were going to do this, we must not have expectations. Actually, it's probably helpful to be downright pessimistic and cynical.

The way this all came about was that we had just received a surprise gift basket from the Sedona Fudge Company. It was probably the best fudge we had ever eaten. We thought, *There's never too much of a good thing; why not take a vacation in Sedona and eat all the fudge we want?*

Why not? And why limit it to fudge?

So, we plotted an all-Arizona food route starting at a Tucson Trader Joe's, then to Envy Bakery, on to Roy's

Hawaiian-fusion restaurant in Chandler (in suburban Phoenix), and ending at the Amara Resort in Sedona, which offers room service from an award-winning chef and hot-stone massages (food for the back) but is also, crucially, located two blocks from the Sedona Fudge Company.

What could go wrong with this? We knew from decades of dashed expectations that anything and everything could go wrong — and probably would. If you haven't noticed, the potential for unpleasantness is infinite.

So, as we took our Prius (our one redeeming attribute) on the road, every few hours of our four-day trip, we asked each other, "How are things so far? Are we enjoying our first vacation in ten years?"

Since these questions were asked against a history of multiple mild to intensely miserable vacations, our expectations were set at zero. Therefore, more often than not, our response was delighted surprise. We had wisely limited our vacation goals. This time our game plan was splendidly simple: gluttony.

The attitudinal consequence of this was that over and over we were surprised to find that not much could bother us. There were incidents, but incidents were expected. Right out of the gate, Trader Joe's was out of our favorite chocolate-chip cookies, and Envy Bakery was closed. But then we remembered AJ's, purveyors of guilt-filled foods.

AJ's, it turned out, had fresh chocolate éclairs, so fresh they had not yet been brought out from the kitchen. They also had some unexpectedly delicious brownies. Car loaded, we were off to Chandler.

At Roy's two things happened that earlier in our marriage might have ruined the evening. First, the table we got was next to a room of Arizona Cardinals cheerleaders, who, I need not remind you, are professionals of loudness. And that night they did honor to their profession. But we reminded ourselves that we weren't there for the ambience; we were there for the food.

Second, the server we had was clearly off her meds. She would lean down, put her mouth inches from your ear, and whisper long indiscernible sentences. But we reminded ourselves that we weren't there to hear the server; we already knew what we wanted to order.

That evening the butterfish was to die for, and the "hot mousse volcano" dessert was worth eternal damnation. Our evening was complete.

Next came Sedona.

Again, we encountered circumstances that before would have put a damper on things. The entire drive through possibly the world's most breathtaking scenery was under construction. There wasn't twenty feet of unobstructed road. But we reminded ourselves that we weren't there for the road; we were there for the food. And the exquisite red-rock formations could still be seen whenever we dared take our eyes off the hundreds of road hazards.

And so it went. Room with a view of the utility court, but room service from a moaningly sumptuous menu. Supercilious resort ducks disdainful of our stale biscuits, but stone massages from old-fogy-sensitive masseuses.

The Sedona Fudge Company had at least a dozen different flavors, a plethora of chocolate candies, and half a display case full of flavorful, fresh-baked cookies. By the time we got back to Tucson, most of the uneaten goodies we had bought were dried out. But that was *after* the vacation. It doesn't count.

The moral of the story is this: make your goal as simple as possible, set your expectations at zero, don't be afraid to be spontaneous, remember that the world doesn't owe you anything, and even dark chocolate has inner light.

Rest

Don't bring up "the issue" when it's time to go to bed. Not even if you're alone. If you can't rest your body, you *can* rest your mind.

Fantasies are fine. They don't have to contain some moral or be spiritually correct. As long as the fantasy is pleasing to the mind, it calms and soothes.

For many people, counting parks the ego. It gives it something to do besides searching for worries and regrets. Simply counting to ten or counting breaths is often enough to settle the mind.

Some people find that breathing as slowly as possible can be helpful. For others, breathing, however it is done, can be accompanied with words. Say, "All released. All is peace." As you breathe out, picture each concern that you are releasing. Then as you breathe in peace, let peace spread throughout your mind and body.

A breathing exercise I find helpful is to repeat, "I drown in God and breathe in peace."

SACRIFICE:
TO MAKE SACRED OR HOLY

The Bible says that before beginning his ministry, Jesus was led by "the Spirit into the wilderness to be tempted of the devil." He then spent forty days fasting in the desert, after which, the Bible says, "he was hungry." (Proving the Bible has a sense of humor.)

Naturally, the devil's first temptation was "If thou be the Son of God, command that these stones be made bread."

Note that the Spirit's *only* stated aim was for Jesus to be tempted. Before he could even begin, Jesus had to confront his ego or dark side or inner demons, or whatever one wants to call the part of us that keeps us in a hell of longing, pettiness, resentment, self-pity, and fear.

In the Christian tradition, Lent is thought of as the forty-day period of self-denial leading up to Easter. And clearly, something must be sacrificed if one's life is not to go in a hundred contradictory directions.

But what to sacrifice? Surely not mere chocolate and TV. The Latin roots of the word *sacrifice* mean "to make sacred or holy." It is clear that in the case of Jesus, his ultimate goal was to make his *mind* holy. He purified his body as a means of gaining clarity of purpose.

However, the more common reason why people make sacrifices is to be a victim and thereby feel innocent. Here is where sacrifice becomes a mistake. For example, in relationships, partners often make grudging concessions while storing up grievances. This form of sacrifice protects their need to be right. They *are* right; it's just that they were nagged, or blackmailed, or shut out until they gave in. Or so they tell themselves.

Unless this pattern is reversed, the couple is eventually buried under a mountain of old resentments to the point where they can no longer view each other with clarity. They decide what is true about the other, and that decision is all they see.

One of the more interesting examples of just what individuals are willing to sacrifice to be right occurred when Gayle and I counseled a couple who had maintained a bitter argument for three years over whether to get married. She was for it. He was not. Go figure.

Knowing that the ego or sentence layer of their minds could not resolve this issue peacefully, we told them to each think of ten things that they liked about the other, recalling specific instances whenever possible, and then tell them to their partner. We knew that this might shift their awareness to a different part of their minds where issues can be solved peacefully.

We had the man start off. His list was so touching that he, and Gayle and I also, had tears in our eyes. When he finished the list, he didn't speak for a moment. Then he said, "Will you marry me?"

The woman immediately stood up. She said, "Now you ask me! After three years! I will never, ever marry you!" And she left.

I wish I could tell you this story ends happily, but it doesn't. She eventually asked him to move out of her house. She had sacrificed the one thing she had told Gayle and me she wanted more than anything else. But like many couples prove each day, what she wanted even more was to be right. And to be right, we must make someone else wrong, *even if that means reversing our position.*

Sacrifice is such a fearful concept for most people that giving up unhelpful mental content is accomplished more easily when the mental patterns being sacrificed are small and manageable. With this in mind, here are some mini exercises that offer the experience of successful cleansing. Just one a day is enough.

1. For one day, say these words about any activity you are engaged in: *This has the meaning for me that I choose to give it.*

2. For one day, when faced with a choice of any kind, ask yourself, *Which would make me feel better about myself?*

3. For one day, judge nothing that occurs.

4. For one day, turn any fear over to God.

5. For one day, pray for one other person.

Every time someone chooses not to judge, every time someone chooses to trust instead of be anxious, every time someone chooses to be kind instead of attack, they turn toward the light.

This has a profound effect on the world. If we could view the world from space, like astronauts with spiritual vision, we would see a light go on every time someone forgave. Someday the world will be blanketed in light, and darkness will be no more. We can hasten that day.

Nothing Is Lost,
and No One Is Far Away

Each thing we have experienced is a door God holds open. "My child, take my hand and walk with me into the embrace of Truth. Let me show you that even then I was with you." Because we are welcomed and that welcome will never cease, nothing is lost and no one is far away.

The Circle of Oneness

It is a mistake to believe that we are somehow greater than the earth, because the earth is a symbol of our oneness. We live on a planet with no beginning and no end, no starting point and no finish. This circle of oneness attracts all things unto itself. We come from it, and we return to it. If we could see the Divine idea behind the earth, we would no longer be afraid.

ONLY LOVE

God is love. In those three words all questions are answered. How do you heal the past? Love. How do you trust the future? Love. How do you see others as they are? Love. What happened before your body began? Love. What happens to you after death? More love. How will the world end? In love.

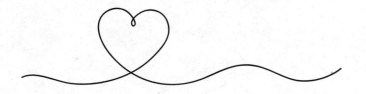

Acknowledgments

I want to thank Joe Durepos for all his amazing work on this book. Not only did he find my email address, but he also worked tirelessly to help me edit and make some changes to the book. It is truly a three-person endeavor, and I know that Hugh also agrees with this.

A Note from Gayle about Her Beloved Husband

Hugh was one of the most caring and loving human beings in this world ... although he, like all of us, also had his ego failings, but he worked hard to correct these through love, peace, and oneness. He was a wonderful father and husband. I want to share one anecdote about his ability to love and care for others. When my mother became ill with an unknown disease that we only learned the name of after her death (progressive supranuclear palsy) and my father could no longer care for her, Hugh said that we should take her to live with us, which we did. This meant that we could no longer travel, which did hurt our "business," but neither one of us was too distressed about that. Here is what was so amazing: Hugh became her primary caretaker because I found it so painful to watch the mind of this extraordinary woman deteriorate until she could no longer speak. He changed her diapers, and gave her showers, and dressed and undressed her. He also talked to her about love, oneness, and peace even though she couldn't respond. He truly made the end of her life not only bearable but even peaceful.

About the Authors

Hugh and Gayle Prather spent most of their forty-five years of marital life as authors and together wrote twenty books. Most of those books had only Hugh's name on them, which Gayle not only accepted but wanted. Being married for so long gave them ample material for their books, as well as for their years of giving workshops, interviews, and free counseling to couples and basically anyone who needed help. They not only learned to love each other eternally — which, given the difficulties they have written about, was not easy — but recognized that forgiveness allowed this to be. Hugh died suddenly in 2010, and Gayle still lives in the house where they spent their last years together. They have two wonderful sons and two amazing grandchildren, and Gayle has a psychotic feral cat that she found and brought home because she knew that no one would adopt her. While Gayle has spent years counseling her, Frances (nicknamed Cheetah) has not changed. Recently Gayle also agreed to take in an elderly cat named Chicken who was sadly declawed before his previous owners adopted him. Cheetah is grateful that he doesn't have claws, and he has the scars to prove this. However, he is an amazingly forgiving cat who thinks he is a dog, which may explain his ability to forgive.